Called to Bless

"*Called to Bless* is a gem in the realm of spiritual literature. This book is a treasure trove of wisdom, filled with poignant testimonies and real-life stories that resonate deeply. What sets it apart is its beautifully simple yet profoundly insightful explanation of the concept of blessing rooted in Scripture. *Called to Bless* will undoubtedly become a handbook for those seeking to embrace this profoundly effective prayer model and transform lives in the process."

—Joseph Acton, North American director, The International Order of St. Luke the Physician

"For anyone who is seeking healing and inner peace, *Called to Bless* offers a simple yet profound means of receiving and giving God's blessing. This book is a powerful resource for people who wish to enrich their lives and the lives of others in their circle of relationships. Through the use of many Scripture passages and personal testimonies, John Rice proclaims the profound truth that we are all called to bless one another in Jesus' name."

—Paul Feider, author of *Living a Transformed Life*

"*Called to Bless* is a reawakening of the Ministry of Blessing, which we are all called to do. John Rice's examples and Scripture verses are easily understood and leave profound examples to follow for how to pray blessings over people. Blessing prayers can remove past hurts and bring us into Christ's new creation. It has done this for me. I pray this book opens the doors for you also."

—Kris Sendelbach, faith caring nurse

CALLED TO BLESS

Restoring God's Ministry of Blessing

JOHN RICE

FOREWORD BY
Russ Parker

RESOURCE *Publications* · Eugene, Oregon

CALLED TO BLESS
Restoring God's Ministry of Blessing

Resource Publications
An Imprint of Wipf and Stock Publishers
199 W. 8th Ave., Suite 3
Eugene, OR 97401

www.wipfandstock.com

PAPERBACK ISBN: 979-8-3852-1895-0
HARDCOVER ISBN: 979-8-3852-1896-7
EBOOK ISBN: 979-8-3852-1897-4

VERSION NUMBER 05/10/24

I dedicate this book to my wife, Debra and to our son, Josh, who have blessed me beyond measure with their loving presence.

Contents

Foreword

IT IS MY HONOR and privilege to write this foreword to John Rice's book especially as we have enjoyed a rich friendship beginning over twenty years ago when we met at the conference of the Fellowship of Christ the Healer of which I was a co-founder. I am especially grateful for our holy nights together at a friend's prayer house in North Carolina where we opened our hearts to one another and prayed for each other.

This is a book with a rich tapestry of applications of the ministry of blessing to a wide range of healing and pastoral needs. It comes complete with a good biblical framing of the power of blessing and a host of testimonies and stories to the impact of blessing. I cannot emphasize enough the important truth that every Christian is called and commissioned by our high king, Jesus, to engage in this ministry of blessing.

My own involvement was born out of frustration and a longing to see my son return to a living faith in Jesus Christ. I had prayed for him for many years but seemingly to no effect. Then one day my son Joel made a statement that blew a hole in my prayer life. He said to me; "Dad, I know when you pray for me even though I am living over a thousand miles away in the Middle East." At first I thought he was flattering me but he went on to say, "I get a headache when you pray for me!" He went on to say that he imagined my aggressive and full on style of praying for him, the lost son languishing in a sort of no-man's-land and he was praying for God to come and get him. At times like this he said he just went into hiding inside of himself until the headache eased.

I was shattered by this revelation. It drove me to seek God afresh and to ask him how then should I pray for my son that would be more effective than this. What the Lord impressed upon me was that I was to bless my son so that his life would flourish in the way God wanted it to. I turned this challenge over and over in my mind and asked God again if he could fine-tune what words I should use for this prayer. What came to me was this statement of blessing intent: "Joel, I bless you to so miss Jesus that you go looking for him until you find him." I opened my study window and called out this blessing to my son who lived far away and across oceans.

Within a year he rang me to say that he had come home to Jesus. I was astonished and grateful to God and wept like a baby. I asked him what had happened and he told me that I would laugh if he told me but tell me he did. He said that he kept waking up in his apartment in Abu Dhabi missing Jesus. He didn't know why but the more he asked himself what was going on the more he reconnected with all those moments when his mother and I tucked him up in bed at night when he was about four years old. He astonished me by saying, "I realized dad that there was a presence in the room and I have only just realized that it was Jesus." And so after years of neglect he came home to his faith in Christ.

My whole prayer life changed as a result of this. So let me commend this book to your reading and encourage you to become the one who blesses others. If we are commissioned by God to anything that commission comes with God's power and authority to do so. So the ministry of blessing comes with divine resourcing and it is therefore not so much a request as a pronouncement of faith and expectation for God to act. And the anticipated outcome of every pronouncement of blessing is that the presence of God comes closer. Remember, the Aaronic blessing is given for the express purpose of God "putting his name back on his people" (Num 6:27). The whole nation had lost its closeness to God through the fiasco of the golden calf. This blessing was restorative and redeeming for the whole nation.

So then, do read this book with the holy intent of learning how to take up your God-given commission to be the one who is called to bless others.

Rev. Dr. Russ Parker

Author of *Rediscovering the Ministry of Blessing*
Founder and Director of 2Restore.

Acknowledgments

LOOKING BACK, I REALIZE that the Lord has been preparing and equipping me to write this book for more than ten years. There have been so many who have been part of that decade-long process—family members, friends, colleagues, and mentors. You have all blessed me and taught me about healing and blessing ministries as you shared the work of God's Holy Spirit in your lives. Thank you for the gift you are to me and to so many others!

My love and thanksgiving for my wife, Debra, runs deeper than I have words to express. Her support, encouragement, and wise suggestions made all the difference in the writing of *Called to Bless*. Also, it was so much fun to co-write the chapter on "Healing and Reconciling God's Creation through Blessing" with her.

As I began writing this book, I felt the Holy Spirit's leading to invite others to send me their blessing stories as a way of making blessing ministry come alive to the reader. Though I was not able to use all those stories due to space constraints, I am deeply thankful to each of you. Your stories will be a source of encouragement and inspiration to all who read this book.

Much of the content in this book arises from the God-sent leadership team at The Blessing Place of Western North Carolina. I am deeply thankful to each of you for your faithful hearts and gifted talents. Together, God continues to use us in restoring his blessing ministry.

To the Rev. Deacon Theresa Blakely, thank you for your chapter on "Blessing Prayers for Church and Community Needs." It adds much depth and breadth in the creative ways we are called to bless. To special mentors and brothers in Christ, the Rev. Russ Parker, Rev. Josh Acton, and Rev. Paul Feider, thank you for the years of deep friendship. Your wise teachings and mentoring have helped me say "Yes" to God in writing and becoming a man called to bless.

Lastly, I give thanks for my faithful companion, Romeo, our family cat. He spent countless hours with me, either curled up on my desk while I was writing or on my lap during times of praying and listening.

Introduction

SEVERAL YEARS AGO, I attended a healing conference where Russ Parker spoke on the topic of blessing. I remember how deeply moved I felt as I listened to the life-changing blessing stories that he shared. I began to understand God's promise to release more of his blessings, more of his goodness and grace, when we bless one another in Jesus' name (Num 6:27). The Holy Spirit convicted my heart with this truth about blessing ministry *". . . for this you were called."* The conviction was so strong that I knew that I was being called to the ministry of blessing. I began by teaching others about God's blessing ministry, relying heavily on Russ' book, *Rediscovering the Ministry of Blessing.*

One of my first teaching opportunities happened at a church in Greenville, South Carolina. Each teaching included a prayer exercise for attendees to practice blessing prayers. It was such a powerful experience of speaking blessings upon others. At the end of that conference, one of their leaders approached me. Jim asked, "John, have you ever read the book, *The Grace Outpouring*?" I told him no. Jim said, "You have to read it. It's all about God's ministry of blessing." Jim gave me a copy of the book which I couldn't put down once I began reading it. Written by Roy Godwin and Dave Roberts, this book quickened my spirit more than any book I had read in many years. The stories shared in *The Grace Outpouring* reveal God's desire to pour out more of his goodness and grace, no matter the situation or need, and how we are all called to be a people of blessing.

My journey in blessing ministry began to grow and expand through an invitation to help restart a healing ministry at High Pastures Retreat Center located near Burnsville, North Carolina. God assembled a team of people intent upon discerning God's vision for this new ministry. As we prayed and listened on Sunday evenings over a seven month period, a healing ministry rooted in blessing began to take form and shape. We called it The Blessing Place of Western North Carolina. We soon learned that healing is always one of God's blessings. At the same time, we discovered that blessing prayers are infused with the power of the Holy Spirit, bringing healing into our lives.

Then came the conviction that God wanted me to write a book on blessing ministry. I asked individuals who had received our blessing ministry training to send me a few of their blessing stories. I knew their stories would make the teachings in this book come alive. At the same time, I began reading *The Power of Blessing* by Kerry Kirkwood. I found myself drawn to his wisdom and insights on blessing ministry, especially how the power of blessing can bridge the gap and separation between individuals caused by our political and theological differences. His book significantly broadened and deepened my understanding of blessing ministry.

We live in a world that seems bent on separating itself into camps of like-mindedness. The resulting divisions create contentiousness, polarization and isolation. The world needs more and more of God's blessing ministry to heal those divisions. You and I are called to be a people of blessing, speaking words of blessing wherever there is community and individual need. Praying the blessing of the fullness of God's intentions into those needs, those situations. Each of us is uniquely created in God's image. This means that no one else can speak blessings as you are created to do. This is why each chapter ends with a few questions for reflection and study. My hope is that these questions will help deepen your understanding of blessing and give you insight as to where to begin or expand your call to God's ministry of blessing.

1

The Story of the Blessing Place of Western North Carolina

"A time to seek, and a time to lose" (Eccl 3:6a)

WE ARE ALL ON a journey. Seventy-three years for me as of this writing and still going pretty strong. One of the consistent threads I've experienced during those years is that God always has more for us. More beauty. More love. More challenges. More learning. More understanding. More ministry. More to receive. More to give away. More and more of God in our lives.

The story of The Blessing Place of Western North Carolina is a story of "God's More." For me, it began during the fall of 2015. My wife, Debra, and I, both Episcopal clergy, had retired a few years earlier from parish ministry. For me, "retirement" was God's way of giving me more time and energy for Jesus' healing ministry. And yes, more time to fish and garden as well. Life was good, filled with blessings. Yet God had more for us.

Sometimes that "more" comes in surprising packages. God often speaks to my wife, Debra, in her dreams. Over the years, we have learned to trust that voice. One morning Deb shared a dream that she kept having over and over again. She said, "I keep hearing God say, *'Turn around and go back the way you came.'*" I asked her

1

how long she had been having this dream. I was stunned when she told me she had been having the dream for two years. I asked her, "Why didn't you tell me sooner?" She said, "Because I knew you weren't ready to hear it. God told me to wait. This morning he said it was time." There are times when Deb's wisdom and her God listening leaves me speechless.

We prayed for understanding of what it meant to "turn around and go back the way you came." At first, we thought that God was telling us to return to one of the places where we had previously lived. There were lots of places to choose from as we had lived in Ohio, Alaska, Vermont, Chicago, and North Carolina. It took a while, but we finally began to understand that God was not calling us to a particular geographical location. Rather, the leading was to return to a spiritual home, to our spiritual roots. For Deb, that meant the Quaker tradition. For me, it was the Wesleyan tradition (United Methodist Church.)

We sensed that this part of our journey meant moving once again. This was not good news as I was already grieving over the coming loss of our beautiful mountain home and friends. I was so upset that Deb finally asked me if I was angry at her. I said, "Yes. I'm angry at you. I'm angry at God. I'm angry at myself for being so angry. I am just angry." Not a good place to be. I knew I needed help.

I called, Kay, a former church member and trusted friend of many years. I shared my struggle with her. After prayerfully listening to my story, she spoke these words, *You just need to trust God!*" Her words of truth reverberated deep in my spirit, bringing a sense of peace.

And so continued our journey of "more," one that I described as a time to seek and a time to lose. Help us Lord, especially me, to let loose of this place, this land, so that we may be free to seek the new place, the "more" you have prepared for us.

Through a series of God events, we found our new home in Burnsville, North Carolina, a small rural mountain town located forty-some miles north of Asheville. The year was 2016. Deb began to settle into her new Quaker community and me into a local

Methodist Church. (Their pastor turned out to be a long-time friend of mine—one of many surprises God had prepared for us.) Throughout that first year in Burnsville, I kept hearing about a local conference center, High Pastures Retreat Center. What was this place? Why did I keep hearing about it?

One afternoon, my pastor friend invited me to go with him to pray for a church member who had been suffering from constant back pain for more than three months. It was one of those God-appointed visits. As we prayed for this godly woman, she began to experience significant pain relief. I still remember what she said when I asked her if she would stand up and walk around the room. "No. I don't want to. I just want to sit quietly in my chair. It has been so long since I've had no pain!" About that time, I heard a loud ripping noise, like Velcro being torn apart. The woman's sister, who had joined us to be part of the prayer team, began giving thanks and praising God, not only for her sister's pain relief, but for her own. As she finished removing a large Velcro wrap from her knee, she said, "My knee has been swollen, causing me excruciating pain for months now. As we were praying for my sister's back, God healed my knee. It doesn't hurt anymore!" We all began to give God thanks and praise! By the way, the husband of the woman suffering from back pain was the Director of High Pastures Retreat Center!

Out of that anointed prayer session came an invitation to do some teaching on Jesus' healing ministry for several groups at High Pastures. Then came the invitation, "John, would you please help us restart a healing prayer ministry here at High Pastures. We've been waiting for several years for God to send someone to do this with us." Once again, I began to see how little we know whenever we say yes to God. This is where trust and faith become so important. When we step out in faith, trusting God's call, his plan for us begins to unfold. Blessing ministry was not even on my radar. It was, however, at the heart of God's plan.

Listening, trusting, and obeying God the best we can will always bear fruit, fruit that we could never have imagined. Pam, a prayer minister and friend, would describe what was happening this way, *"Obedience precedes understanding."* Have you ever said yes to God without having any idea where your yes will take you or what it will look like? Yet by faith, you said, "Yes, Lord." Our listening to and trusting God are key building blocks to our obeying God, to our saying, "Yes, God!" Know that your yes to God is always a yes to receiving and experiencing the "more" that God desires for you. More Joy. More Love. More Light. More Healing. More Peace. More Life!

"Be still before the Lord and wait patiently for him"
(Ps 37:7a)

I shared with several friends that I had been invited to help restart the healing ministry at High Pastures. I knew that God had a vision for this new ministry and I knew we were being called to build it according to God's plan. This would be our priority ... and still is. Oh Lord, let this healing ministry be what you want it to be.

Those friends said yes to joining me in seeking God's vision for the new healing ministry at High Pastures. We would do this together by gathering on Sunday evenings on the beautiful mountainside of the retreat center, to *"be still before the Lord and wait patiently for him."* We would always share with one another what we heard or saw during our waiting upon the Lord prayer time. This would be our prayer discipline for nearly seven months.

During that seven-month period, I was invited to do some teaching on blessing ministry at a church in Greenville, South Carolina. Much of what I taught I had learned from a friend and colleague, Rev. Russ Parker. His book, *Rediscovering the Ministry of Blessing*, is one of the best resources available in understanding the depth and breadth of God's ministry of blessing.

Following the conclusion of this workshop on blessing ministry, Dr. Jim Childs, leader of their church's' healing ministry, walked up to me. He asked, *"John, have you read the book, 'Grace Outpouring' by Roy Godwin and Dave Roberts? Have you heard of Ffald-ye-brenin retreat center in Wales?"* I had not. Jim told me that I had to read the book, especially if I was going to continue teaching on blessing ministry. He gave me a copy of the book and I headed home.

Dr. Childs was right. *Grace Outpouring* was one of those books that I could not put down. It is the story of how the Holy Spirit led the leadership and staff at Ffald-ye-brenin to embrace blessing ministry as the heart of their ministry. It is one of the most inspiring God stories that I had read in many years. I began to quietly wonder if God was revealing what he wanted healing ministry at High Pastures to look like—a ministry of blessing?

I bought copies for every member of our Sunday evening prayer group. We were all drawn to the story of Ffald-ye-brenin and to God's ministry of blessing. As we talked and prayed about the possibilities, excitement grew. This excitement deepened when the director of High Pastures told us that every member of their board had read *Grace Outpouring* two years prior. It is true, "There is an appointed time for everything, a time to seek and a time lose." And that appointed time will be made known to those who "wait upon the Lord."

"And my God will provide all you need" (Phil 4:19).

We were not fully aware of what was happening during those first seven months. Yet there were signs of God's presence every time we gathered on Sunday evenings. Peace, a holy expectation, and words (images) of knowledge were a few of those God signs. Two images, a beautiful rainbow and a river of living water, kept appearing during each prayer gathering. Initially, the rainbow was small, covering just a portion of the retreat center. It was that close, that vivid! However, the more time we spent waiting upon the Lord, the larger the rainbow grew, extending out and over the town of Burnsville, located a few miles away. The rainbow image kept growing in size, extending for miles and miles over the entire area of western North Carolina and beyond.

The image of the river of water also kept getting bigger and bigger. It started out as a spring of water coming down the mountainside of the retreat center. Eventually the spring turned into a stream and then swelled into a river of living water. That river was alive with aquatic plants and colorful fish. Just like the rainbow, the river flowed down into the town of Burnsville and slowly expanded further and further out. It began to cover all of western North Carolina and into neighboring states.

As we talked and prayed about these and other signs, we began to understand God's vision for our healing ministry. We believed that blessing ministry was to be at the heart of our ministry, but we were all so new to blessing prayers. We didn't even know if they could be used as a form of healing prayer. After all, we were being called to help start a healing ministry. We began to ask God, "Lord, do you want to use blessing prayers to bring healing to your people?

Within weeks, God provided the answer through a prayer referral from friends in Asheville. "John, we want to send Ed to you for prayer. There is much trauma and deep hurt in his past. He seems ready to receive more of God's healing. Would you pray with him?" Kim, my prayer partner, and I said yes.

We arranged a quiet and private place at High Pastures to meet and pray with Ed. For nearly an hour, we heard story after story of Ed being abused, neglected, and abandoned during his childhood and young adult years. Much of my thirty years in healing prayer ministry has focused on inner healing (healing the deep hurts of the past). Of the hundreds of individuals that I have prayed with for inner healing, Ed would be near the top of the list of the most traumatized and wounded. There was so much hurt and pain that I wasn't sure where to start praying.

We took a break. I walked and prayed, asking Jesus where do you want to start with Ed's healing? I heard, "John, I don't want you to use the inner healing prayer model where you invite me to come and be with Ed in specific pain-filled memories." I asked, "How do you want us to pray?" Jesus said, "I want you and Kim to pray blessings over Ed. Once you begin, the Holy Spirit will give you the words to speak. You and Kim are to listen for and speak the blessings the Spirit gives you."

I shared this with Ed and Kim. They readily said yes, even though none of us knew exactly what that meant. It didn't come to me at that moment, but it does now. *Obedience precedes understanding! Obedience to Jesus precedes healing!* We began to pray for Ed, inviting the Holy Spirit to lead us. It was to be a life-changing moment for all three of us.

I began to pray with these words, "Ed, in Jesus' name, I bless you with God's love flowing directly from Abba's heart into your heart." (This particular blessing prayer is often where I now begin speaking blessings over individuals.) As Jesus said, words of blessing began to enter my thoughts. It was the Spirit at work. I continued to pray, "Ed, in Jesus' name, I bless you with the Light of Christ pouring out into all those dark places of family violence and abuse, of drugs and alcohol. I bless you with the Light of Christ vanquishing and pushing the darkness far away at this very moment. I bless you with knowing that God has never rejected you nor abandoned you." Kim then began to pray words of blessing. When she paused, I would speak additional blessings that the Holy Spirit gave to me. Then Kim would add more blessings the Spirit gave her to pray. Back and forth the blessings were spoken over Ed, all in Jesus' name.

We prayed blessings into the places of deep hurt and trauma that Ed had shared with us. Our blessing prayers seemed so brief (no more than twelve to fifteen minutes), yet the Spirit's presence was so palpable. Kim and I encouraged Ed to go to the Prayer Tower to simply have some quiet God time. The Prayer Tower is a small silo-type stone structure. It is one of those holy places at High Pastures. When Ed and I arrived, we walked inside and up to the altar. I remember my awkwardness in what to say. I finally blurted out, "Jesus, here's Ed. He's all yours." Ed told us later about the extraordinary healing journey he had with Jesus that began as soon as I left the Prayer Tower. Here is his story in his own words.

Dear John and Kim,

I would like to thank you both for taking your time to meet with me October 5, 2017, for prayer at High Pastures Christian Retreat Center. I certainly felt the presence of the Spirit of God moving throughout our session. What happened next was what I will call a life-changing experience worthy of a written testimony—quiet, healing time with the Lord, our Father, at the Prayer Tower and surrounding areas.

Before I go into my testimony, I believe there is one more thing worth noting—the providential work of the Holy Spirit that led to our prayer session. I can clearly see in retrospect how the Spirit worked through others involved in the healing ministry united in the body of Christ. I am convinced, once again in my Christian walk that this was not coincidence; it was the GRACE of God unfolding.

Now back to the prayer tower story! It did not take long from the time I was dropped off at the prayer tower to the time I was involved in an intimate conversation with God. But this was not like the prayers that we Christians are frequently accustomed to. Our Father did most of the talking as I surrendered to Him.

As I began to pray to the Lord, I presented my requests for any inner healing that may still be needed for the many trials and tribulations I had experienced while in the valley. What happened next was, again, life changing to say the least. I felt as if the Spirit put me in a "trance" and played a video on my "mental screen" of those difficult times, showing me how Jesus was present at every moment during my trials. Wow! He took me back to the beginning when I was in my mother's womb and continued to the present. I found myself, still basking in His presence, standing in the center of the prayer tower. While regressing to the womb and throughout my childhood I was in tears of pain. But, when "awakening" to the present moment I was filled with JOY. At this point, it became a prayer of thanksgiving for the BLESSING I had just received. I turned around, now facing Jesus' "open arms." The beautiful carved wooden arms were reaching out to me within the prayer tower just below the radiant round window which symbolized His Face shining His light onto me. This certainly added to the experience with the realization that I was being embraced with these arms the entire time. I felt FREE and BLESSED! I felt . . . . HEALED! Jesus was basically reminding me of His promises found throughout the inspired Word of God. Then, once again, something interesting began to happen. A more appropriate term may be *supernatural!*

As I continued to experience the JOY of the Spirit, I began to feel a Spirit-led impulse that it was time to leave and go to what became my next destination. I thought the feeling was strange as I initially did not want to leave. This destination turned out to be a walk in the woods along the *Prayer Trail* with my friend Jesus. Oh, *What a friend I have in Jesus!...*, or, *Just a little talk with Jesus makes it right!* . . . as the old hymns go. At this point my talk with Jesus consisted of more audible whispers (on my part) and I felt His leading to every posted scripture on the trail. The experience with my Great Friend had become an *apologetic* one. I was reminded of His creation as I continued to observe what could not have happened by chance. It was majestic! As we came to the end of the trail, I was led back up to the Prayer Tower where I entered once again and spent more time in thanksgiving prayer. As I exited High Pastures with excitement all I wanted to do was share my story, which I did, leading this time to *their* excitement and desire to visit the center.

As I end this letter, I feel as if the words used are not adequate in sharing my experience. But I do hope that they will serve as an appreciation and gratitude on my part. But mostly, I will continue to pray that this testimony serves as a witness to what the Lord can do in the blessing ministry. My wishes are for everyone to experience His presence and work leading to a transforming life-changing experience as we surrender to the LOVE, GRACE, and MERCY that He has in store for us. God is real, and I know He is present at High Pastures!

Thank you for being the hands and voice of God. To God be the glory!

In Christian Love,

Ed

Jesus wanted more for Ed, much more. During Ed's God time in the Prayer Tower and while hiking the nearby Prayer Trail, Jesus talked with Ed, walked with Ed, and healed Ed. Jesus set Ed free. Free from guilt and shame. Free from rejection and abandonment. Free from the lies and deceptions of the enemy. Free to receive the fullness of joy and life that Jesus desires to give us all. Truly, God provides all we need!

God's vision for the new healing ministry was quickly coming into focus. Through Ed's story, the Lord answered our question about using blessing prayers in healing ministry. "Yes," said the Lord! We knew that we were also being called to "Restore God's ministry of blessing." This would become God's vision for our new healing ministry.

The name of our ministry, "The Blessing Place of Western North Carolina," reveals more of God's vision. This blessing ministry was not just for those coming to High Pastures, but for all of God's people. Images of rainbows extending far beyond our sight and a river of living water flowing down the mountainside and spilling out over our region and beyond confirmed this for us. We began receiving invitations from churches and healing groups throughout the country to teach and equip others for God's ministry of blessing. We are just beginning to mentor two church groups who are responding to God's call to create a Blessing Place Ministry in their community. It is an exciting time to be about the work of "Restoring God's ministry of blessing."

We, our Blessing Place Ministry Team, have been so richly blessed with God's goodness and grace these past seven years. As you continue to read this book, I believe the Lord wants you to receive more of his blessings as well. *So in Jesus' name, I bless you with the fullness of Abba's love and joy. And I bless each of you with the excitement of being Called to Bless as you are uniquely gifted to do, in Jesus' name. Amen.*

Questions for Reflection and Study.

These questions can be used for personal reflection or group study. They are intended to assist you in your journey of faith, especially in drawing you closer to Jesus through God's ministry of blessing.

1. What are some of your experiences of "waiting upon the Lord" for direction? For discernment?

2. Can you remember a time when you said *no* to God's calling? What did that feel like?

3. Describe a time when you said *yes* to God's call to a particular ministry. What did that feel like?

4. What are some of your experiences where "obedience preceded understanding?"

2

God's Promise to Bless

"The Lord bless you and keep you;
the Lord make his face shine on you and be gracious to you;
the Lord turn his face toward you and give you peace."

(Num 6: 24-26, NIV)

THESE WORDS, WRITTEN IN the Old Testament Book of Numbers, are known as the Priestly Blessing or the Aaronic Blessing. God gave these words to Moses for a very specific purpose. *"Tell Aaron and his sons, this is how you are to bless the people of Israel."* (Num 6:22-23)

As the Holy Spirit inspired the writing of God's word, so the Holy Spirit continues to bring new revelation, new understanding of God's Word to us today. This enlivening of the Word occurs as we re-read even the most familiar verses, such as Aaron's Blessing. It happened to me a few years ago as I read verse 27 of Numbers 6. How many of you, especially those who know the Aaronic Blessing by heart, can recite the words of verse 27? Not me, at least not nine years ago. But that has all changed. I began to see where God continued to give Moses instructions on how Aaron was to bless the people of Israel in verse 27. This one verse significantly expands our understanding of God's blessing ministry.

"So they will put my name on the Israelites, and I will bless them."

Do you see it? Do you hear God's promise to bless as we pray in God's name? Today, this instruction would be something like this: *"As you bless one another in Jesus' name, I will bless them."*

Here it is, God's promise to release blessings of his goodness and grace as we speak blessings upon one another, in Jesus' name. Praying in this way has changed the way I pray, from prayers of request to prayers of blessing, just as God instructed Moses to pray . . . speaking blessing prayers before God, in his Son's name. It is such a simple, effective, and powerful way for us to pray. Why? Because the Lord is our promise keeper. God always keeps his promise to release more of his goodness, grace, and love whenever we pray blessings in his name!

The following is a paraphrase of a story that Russ Parker shared during a teaching he led on blessing ministry. It is a story of God's promise to release blessings.

Bill and Jenny's Story

Three times a year Russ would go on retreat with a small group of men, all of whom were travelling conference speakers. Their gathering always included the opportunity for each person to share their current story and then receive prayer and anointing.

At one particular meeting we could all tell just by looking at Bill, that something was troubling him. His shoulders were slumped over and his head was bowed. Everything he said was filled with despondency. We asked him, "Bill, what's wrong?"

He answered, "It's my daughter, Jenny. She is eighteen years old. Although she made a commitment to Jesus when she was a young girl, in the last six months or so she has become distant and uncommunicative. Just recently I learned that she is pregnant. I was shocked and disappointed. I have prayed that she will return to her faith and to Jesus, but no matter how often I pray, no matter what I pray, nothing seems to work. My prayers make no difference in her life. I'm about ready to just give up. If I cannot win my daughter for Christ what gives me the right to go out and preach this to other daughters?"

Russ asked Bill if he and the others in the group could pray for him and his daughter. Bill said yes but with no enthusiasm as he was deeply saddened by his daughter's story. Russ shared, "We were led to pray blessing prayers over Jenny. Even though she was not in the room I encouraged everyone to imagine that Jenny was not far away and that we could call down blessings upon her as if she was indeed with us. These are the words we used, 'Jenny we bless you with knowing just how much your heavenly Father loves you. Jenny, we bless you with coming home to Jesus.'"

"We continued to pray blessings over Jenny with great fervor. Actually, we pronounced and shouted them out for about ten to twelve minutes. When we finished our prayers, Bill, still filled with despondency, simply said, 'Thanks guys. That was very nice.'

During the coffee break that followed, Bill went outside when his cell phone rang. It was his daughter, Jenny, calling. She said, 'Dad! Dad, where are you? I'm in the mall in town but I can hear you calling my name. Where are you?' The town she was in was over one hundred miles away! She went on to say, 'Oh Dad, I am so sorry for the pain and heartache that I have caused you. Please forgive me.'"

Russ Parker (Farnham, County Surrey, United Kingdom)

What an amazing moment, a moment of God's promise fulfilled . . . to release more of his goodness and grace and love upon Bill and Jenny, starting as soon as Russ and the other men began to speak blessings upon them in Jesus' name.

Though I am never quite sure of what will happen as a result of praying blessings in Jesus' name, I am always certain that something is happening because God always keeps his promise to bless. Sometimes the result of the blessing prayers are seen within moments, such as happened with Bill and his daughter.

Other times, the results of the blessing prayers may take a few weeks, even months, before a change is noticed. And I'm fairly sure that there are times when we will never be aware of the impact our blessing prayers are having. No matter if results are seen quickly, over a period of time or not at all, we can be confident that God keeps his promise to release blessings when you and I bless one another in Jesus' name!

Here are some other blessing stories that friends have sent me. They are a source of inspiration and encouragement for me. I hope they will be the same for you.

Blessing Church Rooms and Ministries

I'm on staff at a church. We had a new music director and she was frustrated that people did not want to join the choir or handbells. A friend and I walked through the halls of the church one evening and blessed the ministry that occurred in each room. We blessed the choir room and within a few weeks the choir director commented to me that she suddenly was overwhelmed with new choir members and people who wanted to play handbells.

Kim (NC)

Blessing Local Businesses

My friend and I walk daily through our small town and pray. We began praying for all the empty buildings to be filled with businesses that would be a blessing to the community and to the business owners. About a year later, we realized how many new businesses had moved into our town and how few empty buildings there were. Now we pray blessings over all the businesses and our town has been flourishing in recent years.

Kim

Blessing of Grandchildren

I had been on the board of The Blessing Place a couple of years when a dear friend of mine shared with me how she would stand in front of her refrigerator each morning and bless each of her grandchildren with the blessing God gave to Moses and the Israelites in Num 6:24-26. I thought, now why didn't I think of that? It hadn't even occurred to me that I could say a blessing to someone far away by looking at them in a picture. So, the next morning, I started blessing my two grandsons, my son, and my daughter-in-law with Aaron's Blessing. After a couple of times, I tacked on the fruits of the spirit at the end. So, it would go something like this:

> *The Lord Bless you and keep you, The Lord make His Face shine on you and be gracious to you, The Lord turn His Face toward you and bring you Love, Joy, Peace, Patience, Kindness, Goodness, Faithfulness, and Self-Control. In Jesus' name. Amen.*

I would look at each one of them in the eyes on my phone where I had their pictures and repeat the blessing to each one of them every morning. I felt God's presence so powerfully that tears would run down my cheeks when I said the words!

Now, this was during a time in my son's life when he was always busy at work and home, so I hated to bother him about anything. My son had stopped going to church when he graduated from high school and only took his sons to church for a year or two until they stopped again. The boys had grown to elementary school age where their mom and dad weren't taking pictures of every cute move they made any more. On top of that, they live so far away that we only see them once or twice a year at most. My youngest grandson had just started kindergarten that year and it was the beginning of the year when I started saying the blessing prayer over them. After about a week, I received an unexpected, surprise video on my phone from my son who hadn't sent any pictures for what seemed like months. It was my grandson singing a song about the fruit of the Spirit that he had just learned in school—*public* school to boot. The song was "I've Got Peace Like a River."

Each time he sang the word "soul," he would grab his little tummy as if he was trying to squeeze his tiny soul right out of him. Well, you can imagine the love, joy, and peace that was in Meemaw's soul when I saw that video and I have been singing my praises to the Lord ever since!

Brenda (NC)

Questions for Reflection and Study

1. Can you remember a time when a person or group of people spoke blessing prayers over you? What did that feel like?

2. Have there been times when you felt led to bless someone? Can you describe your experience?

3. Was there a particular blessing story in this chapter that you especially liked? Why?

3

"For This You Were Called"
(1 Peter 3:9)

WHEN GOD GIVES A vision for ministry, his vision will always be confirmed in Scripture. Our ministry team was intentional in seeking that scriptural basis for our blessing ministry. As we read and studied Roy Godwin's book, *The Grace Outpouring*, the story of God's blessing ministry coming alive at Ffald-ye-brenin retreat center in Wales, we were drawn to two specific scriptural references. Aaron's Blessing (Num 6:22-27) as mentioned in Chapter 1, became a key scriptural basis for the ministry of The Blessing Place of WNC. The second scriptural reference, 1 Pet 3: 9, provided us with the exciting Spirit filled direction for our new ministry:

> *Do not repay evil for evil or abuse for abuse; but, on the contrary, repay with a blessing. It is for this that you were called—that you might inherit a blessing.* (1 Peter 3:9)

Perhaps like you, I had read this Scripture many times over the years. Clearly, we are instructed not to repay evil for evil or abuse for abuse. We are not to repay gossip with gossip, or acts of unkindness with unkindness, or hate with hate. The Word says repay such acts with blessing. But the phrase *"It is for this you were called"* had never really impacted my heart.

As I read *Grace Outpouring* for the first time, I felt as if the Holy Spirit was giving me a new understanding, an awakening to a fuller meaning of 1 Pet 3:9. Blessing ministry is meant to be an important part of our discipleship as followers of Jesus. As disciples of Christ, you and I are called to God's ministry of blessing. Note that this call has no qualifying conditions attached to it. It doesn't say, you are called to bless others if you have extra time or if you feel up to it or when you remember to do it. No. The Word says, *"For this you were [are] called!"*

One more important learning came to us as we studied,1 Pet 3: 9. The meaning of the very last words in the verse, *"that you might inherit a blessing,"* became clear. Whenever we are being led to speak blessing prayers, Scripture says that we will receive a blessing. How wonderful. Not only will God release blessings when we speak words of blessings, God will bless us as we bless others. As a gardener, the image of a soaker hose helps me understand what happens. If you are a gardener, you know that a soaker hose carries water to your flower beds and vegetable garden, "leaking" out droplets of water at the base of the plants where the roots can take it up. As this happens, the soaker hose itself becomes saturated with water. I think this is what happens when we speak blessing prayers upon one another. We are the Lord's soaker hose. Blessings are released exactly where God intends them, upon others as well as us. Here is a story that describes what can happen when we bless one another.

A Family Healing Story

A few years ago, I was teaching on healing ministry at a church in Florida. I taught about the healing power of forgiveness during the opening session on Friday evening. It was a holy prayer time as conference attendees opened their hearts to God's grace, empowering them to speak words of forgiveness, releasing them from deeply rooted feelings of unforgiveness, anger, and judgmental thoughts.

As we were getting ready to leave the church that night, Carolyn, a retired clergy person came up to me in tears. "I've tried many times to forgive my daughter-in-law and my son for abandoning me, but it isn't working. They've not spoken to me in two years and they live just a few miles from my home. I know I need to forgive them. But no matter what I pray and how often I pray to ask God to help me forgive, nothing seems to happen. I just can't seem to get rid of all the anger and resentment and bitterness, especially towards my daughter-in-law. My heart aches. I know I need help. What can I do, John?"

As I was listening to this heart-wrenching story, I began to wonder what could I say that would be of any comfort, that would make any difference to her? I began to ask God what to say to Carolyn. "Tell her the story of Bill and Jenny," is what I heard.

So, I shared the story and began to encourage Carolyn to pray blessings over her son and daughter-in-law when she got home that evening. I encouraged her to pray blessings, in Jesus' name, and to listen to the Holy Spirit for additional words of blessing to speak. "And Carolyn, if you live in an area where you can shout out your blessings without a neighbor calling 911, do that." She agreed.

The next morning, I was visiting with friends in the church parish hall while waiting for the morning session to begin. Carolyn walked into the room and I could tell just by looking at her that something had happened. Her whole demeanor had changed. Her face glowed and she walked like a person no longer weighed down by a heavy burden. She came up to me and said, "I shouted out my blessing prayers last night. I haven't received a phone call from my son yet, but something miraculous happened as soon as I began to bless him and my daughter-in-law. All the anger and resentment and bitterness and unforgiveness that I've been carrying, it all began to melt away as soon as I began to speak blessing prayers!"

What a wonderful story of God's mercy and compassion. For Carolyn, the only difference between the past two years and the previous evening was her saying yes to speaking blessing prayers over her son and daughter-in-law. As she did so, the chains of unforgiveness fell off. All the toxic feelings associated with the unforgiveness "melted" away. Most importantly, Jesus healed Carolyn's broken heart as she prayed blessings over those that had deeply hurt her.

Carolyn's story confirms the truth of 1 Pet 3:9. Repay with a blessing. For this you and I are called. And when we speak blessings, we will inherit a blessing. Carolyn received/inherited God's blessing. For the first time in over two years, she was free from all the emotional garbage connected to her unforgiveness. It was a moment of rejoicing and giving God thanks and praise. Thank you, Lord, for promising to release more of your blessings when we choose to speak blessings upon one another in Jesus' name!

Questions for Reflection and Study

1. Reflect upon the words of 1 Pet 3: 9. What words or phrases capture your attention?

2. Have you ever experienced being blessed as you blessed someone else through blessing prayers or acts of kindness? What did that feel like?

3. Does Carolyn's story remind you of a relationship where you (or a friend) have been deeply hurt by someone you loved and trusted? Have you been able to forgive them? If not, I encourage you to speak blessings upon that individual, upon that situation over and over again, in Jesus' name. And get ready to receive a blessing yourself.

4

"The Holy Spirit Will Teach You Everything" (John 14:26)

JESUS GATHERED THE DISCIPLES in the Upper Room and began to wash their feet. Together they shared the bread and wine of the Last Supper. An important conversation followed their meal. Jesus told his disciples that he will be with them but a little while longer. Where he is going they cannot come, at least not now, *"but you will follow later."* (John 13: 36.) Jesus then gave them a new commandment, *"that you love one another as I have loved you."* (John 13:34) Jesus' journey to the cross is drawing closer. Jesus wanted his disciples to understand what is about to happen, preparing them for his death and resurrection. He lets them know that though his public ministry will end soon, theirs is about to begin.

This is the setting for Jesus' message as recorded in the gospel of John, chapter 14. Here, Jesus shared foundational teachings the disciples would need in order to continue his ministry of healing and reconciliation: *"Do not let your hearts be troubled. Believe in God, believe also in me."* (v1) *"I am the way, the truth, and the life."* (v6) *"Whoever has seen me has seen the Father."* (v9b) *"The one who believes in me will also do the works that I do and, in fact, will do greater works than these . . . "* (v12) *"When I go, you will not be left all alone: I will come back to you."* (v18, 16)

Jesus wanted to be sure the disciples were listening. These teachings would be vitally important for their ministry. Jesus said, *"I have said these things to you while I am still with you."* (v25) He reminded them again that he would be with them, even though he would be in a different place. How? Through the indwelling presence of the Holy Spirit. *"But the Advocate, the Holy Spirit, whom the Father will send in my name, will teach you everything, and remind you of all that I have said to you."* (John 14:26)

These teachings also speak to modern-day disciples. We too are called to listen urgently to the Holy Spirit and to Scripture. This chapter describes much of what the Holy Spirit has been teaching us at The Blessing Place of WNC, beginning with a focus on listening.

The Importance of Listening

The word listen is derived from the Latin word *discernere*, the same root word for discernment. *Discernere*, not surprisingly, means to listen. It also means a willingness to be taught. When we pray for discernment, we are intentionally listening for the Lord's teaching or leading. It all happens through the power of the Holy Spirit dwelling within us. It is no surprise that Jesus specifically mentions teaching as a main role of the Holy Spirit in our lives.

Hundreds of verses and stories, where listening is a key element, abound in Scripture. One of my favorites comes from 1 Sam 3: 1-10, a story about young Samuel, apprentice to Eli, the temple priest. It is night. Samuel is lying down in the temple when he hears a voice calling, *"Samuel! Samuel!"* Samuel runs to Eli, thinking his mentor was calling him. Eli said, *I did not call you, lie down."* The same thing happens a second and third time. Eli finally realizes (discerns!) that the Lord was the one calling the boy and tells him what to say if God calls out to him again, *"Speak, Lord, for your servant is listening."*

"Now the Lord came again and stood there, calling as before, 'Samuel! Samuel!'" And Samuel said, "Speak, for your servant is listening" (v10B).

I have often wondered why young Samuel does not recognize that it is the Lord who keeps calling him. The Lord had come and was standing where Samuel was sleeping, *"in the temple of the Lord, where the ark of God was"* (v10a) It is further confirmed in Samuel's choice of words in response to God calling him. Eli instructs Samuel to say, "Speak, Lord, for your servant is listening." Note that Samuel does not refer to him as Lord. He only says, "Speak, for your servant is listening" (v3). The Lord is standing right beside Samuel and calling out to him, yet the young apprentice does not know who he is. How can this be?

I believe the answer lies in 1 Sam 3:7: *"Now Samuel did not yet know the Lord, and the word of the Lord had not yet been revealed to him."* Samuel does not recognize the Lord because he has not met him. There is no personal relationship between Samuel and the Lord. And just like us, Samuel would not recognize a voice that he had not heard before.

Another familiar biblical story about listening and voice recognition can be found in John, chapter 10. Jesus tells the story using images of sheep (us) and their shepherd (Jesus). *"The one who enters by the gate is the shepherd of the sheep. The gatekeeper opens the gate for him, and the sheep hear his voice. He calls his own sheep by name and leads them out. When he has brought out all his own, he goes ahead of them, and the sheep follow him because they know his voice"* (John 10: 2-4). This time the voice is "known" because a relationship already exists between the sheep and their shepherd.

This imagery of sheep knowing their shepherd's voice would be easily understood by the people in Jesus' time. It was a common practice for large flocks of sheep to graze the same pastureland during the daytime. Thousands of sheep from different flocks would become all mixed together as they grazed. Each shepherd would have constructed his own simple corral where his sheep would stay overnight, protected from predators and other dangers. What most would consider an almost impossible nightly task for each shepherd, that of gathering the sheep of his flock from amongst the thousands of other sheep, was easily accomplished. The sheep recognized the voice of their own shepherd. The shepherd would call out to them, and like Jesus said, the sheep would follow their shepherd's voice, all the way into their corral. When we know Jesus as our Shepherd, we too recognize his voice and follow him.

Several years ago, I experienced first-hand the importance of knowing the shepherd's voice and how difficult it is to get animals to follow you if they don't recognize your voice. I was completing my graduate studies at the University of Vermont in adult education and animal sciences. Part of my hands-on work included interning on a family run dairy farm, just outside of Burlington, all in preparation to become a County Extension Agent (dairy farm consultant). I would arrive at the farm at 7:00 in the morning to finish the morning milking. Ken, who owned and operated the farm, would then move onto other chores. The summer was filled with many surprising moments. One of those surprises was how natural the work and rhythm of dairy farm-ing came to me. Ken must have noticed because I still remember when he came up to me and said, "John, my wife and I haven't been on a vacation in ten years. We're planning on taking a long four-day weekend in a couple of weeks. The farm will be all yours to operate. Think you can handle it?"

He seemed to be considerably more confident in my abil-ity then I was. However, we moved forward with his plan, which meant I needed to be at the farm by 5:00am every day the fol-lowing week to learn all that was needed to run the farm from sunup to sundown. That first early morning visit brought another surprise. Barn boots and jacket on, Ken said "let's go get the cows and bring them into the barn." That time of year the sixty-five milking cows were turned out onto a nearby pasture for the night. Ken stood at the open bay end of the barn and began shouting, "Come on! Come on girls! Come on!" That's all it took. Every cow slowly began to lumber to the barn in single file. They knew their "shepherd's" voice and they followed him into the barn where they would be milked and fed. I was mightily impressed.

My turn would come a few days later. I couldn't wait to see the cows coming into the barn as I called out to them. The morning arrived. It was a beautiful cool starry night. I stood at the end of the barn and called out, "Come on, come on girls, come on." Nothing. Not even a head turn. I called out to them again and again. A few looked in my direction, but not a single cow took a step towards the barn. Somewhat exasperated and greatly disappointed in their complete lack of response to my "Come on girls," I had to go out into the pasture and literally try to push a number of cows to get them started in. No easy task as a Holstein cow can easily weigh one thousand to twelve hundred pounds.

I'm sure you probably have this figured out by now. The cows didn't respond to my calling out to them because they simply did not recognize my voice. It was not the voice of their "shepherd." It was not Ken. I'm not sure that cows can think, but I can easily imagine them wondering, "Who is this guy calling us? We don't know him." I am happy to say that by the third morning, they began to recognize my voice and slowly lumbered into the barn all on their own. Oh, happy days!

Most of us experience many voices coming at us every day: family, friends, fellow workers, even our own inner voice breaking into our awareness as a simple thought. For example, I'll be driving home and the thought comes, "Don't forget to stop and pick up some milk and bread." Or, "Remember to call your sister to see how she is doing." We all experience such thoughts. I believe this is how Jesus most commonly speaks to us, through thoughts coming into our awareness. These thoughts will reveal the working of the Holy Spirit within us, especially as we listen for the leading of the Holy Spirit, the one sent to teach us and lead us in all things. The more time we spend with Jesus, the deeper our relationship is with him, and the easier it becomes to recognize our shepherd's voice.

Years ago a close friend, Fr. Jim, helped me understand the importance of what I now call relational listening. It is a desire to listen intently to others and have others listen intently to us, that we both may be heard. Relational listening takes time and commitment, resulting in closer relationships. This is what Jesus wants. He wants to be in a close personal relationship with each of us. Jesus describes the relationship like this: *"I do not call you servants any longer, because the servant does not know what the master is doing; but I have called you friends, because I have made known to you everything that I have heard from my Father"* (John 15:15). Here is a story of how Fr. Jim practiced relational listening with Jesus.

Jim and I were both serving as pastors of churches in northern Vermont. We often met for a time of fellowship over breakfast. I still remember the time I asked him what the TCIB on his license plate meant. The best I had come up with was, "To Christ I belong." I really liked that, but he said, "Nope. That's not it." So, I asked, "Well, what does it mean?" Here is what this wise and godly man replied, "It means Take Chair Insert Behind!"

I laughed and laughed, mostly because I knew he was serious. He began to talk about how every morning, he would take a cup of hot tea and muffin and sit down in his lounge chair for a time of prayer and devotions. He described this as his time to simply be with Jesus, listening for the very quiet thoughts or whispers that would come to him from the Lord. He said he would always ask Jesus a question, such as, "Who in my parish needs me to stop by for a visit or phone call today?"

Most days a name or two would come to him, someone who he had no idea was needing pastoral care. He would call or stop by to visit the individual, discovering the struggle they were going through. I began to do the same for my parishioners. Names came, not every day, but quite often. I learned to be very intentional with this new spiritual discipline, listening for the leading of the Holy Spirit. This practice even carried over into my sermon preparations, listening to Jesus for what he wanted me to share with my Sunday congregation. Sometimes, I heard very little. Most times though I received a word or image that became the focus for the message. Those sermons became so much better, so much more meaningful. I remember saying, "Thanks be to God!" I imagine the congregation was saying the same.

A Royal Priesthood

God instructs Moses to appoint his older brother, Aaron, as Israel's first high priest (see Sir 45:6-22). Aaron acted primarily as a mediator between the people and God. Within this sacrificial and centuries old Judaic tradition, the high priest would carry out the role of mediator. They would do this by entering the sanctuary, taking the blood of sacrificed animals, to atone for the sins of the people. Aaron would also take on the priestly role of speaking God's blessings over the people of Israel, as mentioned in Chapter 2.

In our Christian tradition, we believe Jesus is our high priest. He is our mediator. "... *He is the atoning sacrifice for our sins, and not for ours only but also for the sins of the whole world*" (1 John 2:2). As our high priest, Jesus continues to be our mediator, the one "*who is at the right hand of God, who indeed intercedes for us*" (Rom 8:34; Heb 7:25).

What does this have to do with blessing ministry? It's about being called to bless and the authority God gives us to bless. It's about recognizing the status of all believers, what Peter describes as "*a royal priesthood*" (1 Pet 2:5, 9). In Revelation, John writes about Jesus making us into a kingdom of priests to serve God (Rev 1:6). He specifically mentions that our serving God is to be here on earth (Rev 5:10).

As a pastor, I have experienced the role of mediator and intercessor. Yet, according to Scripture, there is more, much more. As a follower of Jesus, you and I are members of God's royal priesthood, called to "*let yourself be built into a spiritual house, to be a holy priesthood . . .* " (1 Pet 2:5). As we grow and mature into our role as a member God's holy priesthood, Jesus gives us power and authority. He sends us "*out to proclaim the kingdom of God and to heal*" (Luke 9:2), to "stand between the holiness of God and the needs of the community."[1]

Speaking blessings, in Jesus' name, fulfills Luke's mandate. When we speak blessings over one another the kingdom of God is

---

1. Parker, *Rediscovering the Ministry of Blessing* (London: SPCK, 2014), 37.

being proclaimed! When you and I speak blessings, the kingdom of God draws near and the healing power of Jesus is released. Blessing ministry is an ancient tradition, yet it feels new. It is a "new way" to proclaim the kingdom of God and to heal. We are literally rediscovering and restoring the call to speak blessings in Jesus' name upon God's people and upon the needs of our communities.

The following story reveals what can happen when we choose to speak blessings upon one another.

The Story of Blessing A Friend's Son

Gloria told me you are looking for blessing stories for your new book. Here are a couple of instances where Gloria's blessing has helped me and my family live more fully in God's love.

When I had not heard from my son for a long time: not knowing where he was, if he was working, and whether he was well—he had been engaged in unhealthy behavior for quite a while; Gloria stood up during prayer group with her arms in the air, and blessed him in the name of Jesus, to bestow on him God's intention for well-being throughout his life. He called me the very next day to say that he was hanging in there.

A couple of months later in my side yard, after praying about my son not working and upon her leaving, Gloria automatically put her head up, looked to the heavens and blessed him in Jesus' name to find and have a job. Three days later, he called to say that his old employer had phoned and wanted him to come back to work!

Praise God that He works His blessings through people like Gloria who believe that this is what God intends them to do, full stop.

Carolyn

"*A Yes On Earth Is A Yes In Heaven*"
(Matt 16:19—The Message)

I have read that the word bless, and its other forms (like blessed and blessing) appears four hundred and ten times in the Bible. That number seemed a little high to me, so I decided to check it myself using my old seminary concordance, which lists by verse every time a word appears in Scripture. I actually counted four hundred and twenty-eight times where the word "bless" and its other forms were used. I was curious, so I did a similar search for the word forgive and its other forms (forgiven, forgiveness, etc.) The theme of forgiveness appears one hundred and forty-three times in the Bible.

How interesting that the theme of blessing appears almost three times more often than forgiveness. I know that it would be an over-simplification to say that blessing holds greater importance than forgiveness based upon these numbers. However, a simple yet significant conclusion can be stated. We are a people called by God to bless and to forgive one another (including ourselves!) again and again.

Just like with forgiveness, we are given a choice . . . . to bless or not to bless. Jesus talks about our choice in this way, *"Whatever you bind on earth will be bound in heaven, and whatever you loose on earth will be loosed in heaven"* (Matt 16:19). The Message translation brings even greater clarity, *"A yes on earth is yes in heaven. A no on earth is no in heaven."*

Obviously, we have no control over God. God does as God wishes. God has, does, and will pour out blessings upon all of creation, including you and me, as God desires. Yet, and here comes part of the mystery of God's ways, we are entrusted by God with whether or not some of his blessings are loosed on earth and in heaven . . . or not. Is this not what Jesus is saying to his disciples? Our yes to speaking blessings on earth (in Jesus' name!) results in blessings being released in heaven and on earth.

The image I have is a river of God's blessings, God's goodness and grace, flowing from heaven to earth. Is it possible that our yes on earth, our speaking blessings, literally opens floodgates in heaven, where God's river of blessings is released upon earth? According to God's Word, I believe the answer is an unwavering yes! And when we say no to being a people of blessing, we must be aware of the consequences. In Jesus words, *"[our] no on earth is a no in heaven."* Our no means those specific "blessing flood gates" of heaven remain closed, holding back the river of additional blessings God desires to pour out upon us. The following is a story of what can happen when we choose to bless in a difficult situation.

The Story of Blessing A Boss

When my son David announced he was leaving his job for a new company and career direction, his boss took it personally and started to create a negative narrative in the office about David. David and I prayed together for his boss and blessed him to see David's new opportunity as a win for both of them and to give David his blessing. The very next day, David received the most supportive email from his boss giving him his blessing and seeing David's good news as a reflection of his leadership in David's life. This was David's first job out of college and his boss was an important mentor to him. Instead of spreading negativity, his boss ended up giving him a special award, many accolades, and blessings before he left.

Tara (Florida)

God's blessings is always part of God's "more" (as discussed in Chapter 1.) The "more" that comes with being a people of blessing will often not be released, by God's own design, without our first saying "yes," yes to God's call to bless. When we say yes, God will release more and more of God's goodness and grace here on earth, replacing despair with hope, darkness with light, loneliness with belonging, fear with love. What is loosed on earth is loosed in heaven!

My friends, I bless you now with a holy boldness in saying "yes" to God's call to blessing ministry. I bless you with God's river of blessing flowing directly from the throne room of God into your homes, your family, your neighborhood, your church, and . . . into your heart! In Jesus' name. Amen.

Freedom from personal agendas

One of the great gifts of blessing ministry is the freedom to pray without any human agenda attached. In our human thinking, there is a tendency to think that we know what is best for ourselves and for others. Sometimes we do, but so often our prejudices and differing world views cloud our understanding of what is really happening around us. Paul said it this way, *"For now we see in a mirror dimly, but then face to face. Now I know in part; then I shall know fully, even as I have been fully known"* (1 Cor 13:12). Paul confirms that our human thinking is incomplete, partial seeing (understanding) at best. But, this all changes in our face to face relationship with Christ, where we begin to see and know fully. The Message puts it this way, *"We don't yet see things clearly. We're squinting in a fog, peering through a mist. But it won't be long before the weather clears, and the sun shines bright! We'll see it all then, see it all as clearly as God sees us, knowing him directly just as he knows us!"*

When I begin to speak blessing prayers, it feels as if I am stepping out of the mist of my human understanding and stepping into the brightness of the Son where I can see more clearly and know more fully. I am not sure how this happens, but I am certain it is the working of the Holy Spirit. Remember, as we bless "we receive a blessing" . . . a blessing of being drawn into the presence of Jesus, "face to face." His presence frees us from our biases and limited understanding. No longer are we squinting in a fog. The weather has cleared and the sun is shining. The Holy Spirit empowers our listening to Jesus who will give us words of blessings to pray, words that are filled with clarity and wisdom and compassion far beyond what we could come up with on our own.

Questions for Reflection and Study

1. Can you think of times when you experienced the specific leading of the Holy Spirit? What was that like for you?

2. Jesus desires a deep personal friendship with each of us. What keeps you from moving deeper in your relationship with him?

3. This chapter focused on several key points about blessing ministry. Did any of these key points speak to you personally?

5
God's Living Hope

TEACHING AND EQUIPPING OTHERS for God's ministry of blessing is one of the most life-giving gifts we can be given. Whenever we are led to teach and pray blessings, I am certain that God the Father, Son, and Holy Spirit are at work in the words of blessing we speak. Jesus is always the life-giving source. Paul writes, *"Now to him who by the power at work within us is able to accomplish abundantly far more than all we can ask or imagine"* (Eph 3:20). Blessing prayers invariably release new life upon the person being blessed and the person speaking the blessings. For many, a renewed hope is at the heart of their new life in Christ.

Peter describes this new life as God's living hope. *"Blessed be the God and Father of our Lord Jesus Christ! By his great mercy he has given us a new birth into a living hope through the resurrection of Jesus Christ from the dead"* (1 Pet 1:3). In Christ, a new living hope is birthed into the world, places where faltering hope exists in our lives.

I believe most of us know what faltering hope feels like in the face of overwhelming life situations, either through our own experiences or those of a close friend. How many of us have prayed again and again for a loved one with a serious illness and seen little to no change? How many of us have prayed for months and even years for their prodigal daughter or son to return home, and they remain lost? Praying for a family struggling financially and matters only get worse? Continuous prayers with no signs of change often lead to self-doubt and faltering hope, like what Bill was experiencing with his daughter Jenny (Chapter 2).

Feelings of hopelessness and powerlessness are on the rise in the world today. It is in our face as we listen to the evening news, news filled with senseless shootings in our schools and on our streets, in our shopping centers and local theaters, and even in our churches, synagogues and mosques. All are signs of a systemic illness and brokenness, so powerful that we can easily feel overwhelmed and powerless. However, no matter the depth of our despair and hopelessness, the truth is, in Christ we are never powerless! Jesus always brings his living hope and resurrection power into the worst of our brokenness and suffering. To think otherwise plays right into the hands of Satan, *"the thief who comes only to steal, kill and destroy"* (John 10:11) the very hope Jesus gives us.

What can we do in the face of such overwhelming life situations, where we feel (and are!) so out of control? Though I do not have the wisdom to answer this question fully, I do know one simple and effective way of bringing light into the darkness of this world. Seek God's help to restore and rekindle God's ministry of blessing, beginning with yourself and your household (or perhaps you and your small prayer group!) Once the fire of blessing ministry has been rekindled in your heart, ask God to help you spread blessing ministry into your church, your healing group, your places of work, your social gatherings, and throughout your local community. It is such a powerful way to bring about life-giving transformation into the world and into our lives.

Healing of a Relationship (brother and sister)

One of the areas where I frequently see God giving birth to a new living hope is in estranged relationships between family members. I hear heart-wrenching stories of deeply conflicted relationships wherever I go to speak. For example, several years ago, I was invited to present a blessing ministry workshop at a church in Alabama. Following one of the teachings, Alice, a middle-aged woman shared the following story with me.

Alice and her brother had always been very close until about three months ago. They had a heated argument. Angry words were spoken, resulting in a very strained and conflicted relationship. Ever since that argument there had been no visits, no phone calls, no interaction at all. She said, "My heart aches. I pray every day, yet my prayers seem to make no difference. I'm not ready to give up, but I just don't know what to do. Then I heard you speak about blessing prayers. I felt the Spirit calling me to use blessing prayers for my brother and myself."

Several weeks later I received an email from Alice with the rest of the story. "John, as soon as I began to speak blessing prayers over my brother things began to change. The change started with me as my anger towards my brother and towards myself began to disappear. Within a few days he called! He didn't even know about my blessing prayers. Our words of anger were replaced with words of forgiveness. Healing and reconciliation happened between us. I am so thankful to God for the gift of blessing prayer ministry."

Alice described her initial prayers as making no difference as far as she could tell. Blessing prayers offered her a new way to pray, a way filled with renewed hope for healing and reconciliation. When she began to speak blessing prayers over her brother, she began to experience God's promise to release his goodness and grace. Blessings filled with the power of the Holy Spirit quickly began to give birth to a new living hope for healing and for a new life between brother and sister. What an amazing hallelujah moment. Thank you, Lord!

This story, and many others, reveal the power of blessing prayers to heal relationships with those we love, as well as with those we do not. For blessing prayers are like the sun and rain as written about in Matt 5:45: *"For the Father makes his sun shine on good and bad people alike, and he sends rain to the righteous and the unrighteous alike."* These words reveal the Father's heart, to pour out blessings upon the righteous and unrighteous alike.

God desires to bless all his people, not just those that agree with our way of thinking. Not just those who worship the way we worship. Not just those of similar economic status. Not just those who share the beauty of a particular skin color. God yearns to pour out more and more of his goodness and grace upon all of humankind. By God's own design, God seeks to do this through our *yes* to being a people called to bless in Jesus' name!

In my own experience and those of hundreds of others, Spirit-filled blessing prayers bring about an awakening within us. It is an awakening for most of us to a "new" way to pray, a way of experiencing firsthand how Jesus brings a new living hope where hope has been waning, where our old ways of praying, sometimes over months and even years, seem to have little to no effect. Jesus is calling out to us at this very moment, *"Sleeper Awake,"* awaken in us to the reality that, *"in Christ, all things are possible."* May our prayerful response be filled with a bold invitation, "Come Holy Spirit, restore within me God's ministry of blessing!"

Unbelief—an obstacle to hope.

I have served as a spiritual director for many Christian renewal weekends known as Cursillo in the Episcopal and Roman Catholic traditions. "Obstacles to Grace" has always been one of my favorite talks to give. Several years ago, I asked Jesus if there were any additional obstacles that I needed to include in my talk. As I listened, I heard the word unbelief. I began to see more clearly how unbelief is a significant obstacle to grace and hope.

I asked Jesus to teach me more about unbelief. I remember being surprised at how quickly his words came. *"Unbelief is a form of spiritual amnesia, revealing that my people have forgotten their true identity as My beloved daughters and sons."* I was nearly overwhelmed by these words as they carried such profound wisdom and truth.

The teaching continued as the Spirit reminded me of a story that a friend had shared with me. Ann, a faithful member of a local Episcopal church, was pregnant with her second child. The baby's room was fixed up with a fresh coat of paint and a new crib. Excitement abounded in all, including their four-year-old son, as they awaited the arrival of their newest family member. Here is where the story becomes very interesting.

The birthing went well. Ann and her husband brought their baby daughter to her new home. About two months later Ann noticed her son walking down the hallway towards his baby sister's bedroom. She and her husband didn't say anything but quietly followed to see what was happening. They saw him walk quietly into her room and over to her crib. He slowly lifted an arm through one of the crib slats and gently began patting his sister on her back. Ann then heard her son whisper these words to his baby sister, *"It's been so long I've almost forgotten. Would you remind me of what heaven is like?"* Here it is. Here is what the beginning of spiritual amnesia in a four-year-old sounds like.

A few months later, I shared Ann's story with Dennis and Sheila Lynn, two of God's most gifted teachers of Jesus' healing ministry. I will always remember their words. "John, you know we have led healing conferences throughout the United States and several countries in South America for many years now. We have heard Ann's story dozens and dozens of times, and each time it has been with a different family!"

If this story was limited to only Ann's family, it would still be food for thought, but perhaps not much more than that. However, when we realize that this story has been experienced by hundreds of different families residing throughout this country and South America, then we must be attentive to what is being revealed at a deeper spiritual level.

First and foremost, I believe these family stories reveal our true identity. We are spiritual beings, known and cherished by God before we were ever formed in our mother's womb. In our human being form, we seem to have a very limited time span in remembering that we are God's beloved daughters and sons, even when we are born into a loving and nurturing family like Ann's. Could it be that in our humanness, our capacity to remember the fullness of life as a spiritual being, including who and whose we are, becomes dramatically reduced? Ann's son is only four years old, yet he says, "It's been so long, I've almost forgotten." You and I know that four years is a short span of time, especially in early childhood. This story reveals how spiritual amnesia begins to have influence in our lives at a very early age.

Thankfully Jesus wants and intends to help us. He speaks directly to our memory banks in John 14:26: *"But the Helper, the Holy Spirit, whom the Father will send in my name, he will teach you all things and bring to your remembrance all that I have said to you."* Jesus wants to restore our memory files. "Come, Holy Spirit. 'It's been so long, I've almost forgotten. Remind me of what heaven is like.' Oh Lord, remind us that we are yours, your cherished and beloved children. Amen."

Blessing ministry is one of God's antidotes to our spiritual amnesia. The blessings of God's goodness and grace and love reminds us who and whose we are . . . awakening us to our true identity as God's beloved daughters and sons.

Blessing Prayer

In Jesus' name, I bless you with a fresh in-filling of the holy Spirit, blessing you with a deep awakening and knowing in your heart that you are God's beloved daughter/son. I bless you with receiving the fullness of God's forgiveness. I bless you with the living hope of Christ in all areas of your life. In Jesus' name I bless you with these words from Romans, "May the God of hope fill you with all joy and peace in believing, so that you may abound in hope by the power of the Holy Spirit." Amen!

Questions for Reflection and Study

1. Are there situations in your life where you are feeling powerless or where hope is fading? If so, is God calling you to speak blessing prayers into those situations?

2. Are you currently facing a relationship that has become strained or conflicted? Where you have prayed and prayed and nothing seems to change? If the answer is yes, ask Jesus to help you begin speaking blessing prayers into that relationship.

3. Are there places in your spiritual journey where you have struggled with unbelief? What is causing that struggle? Ask Jesus to help you surrender all this to him.

6

Blessings, Curses and Reconciliation

The Power of Blessing

"*I* CALL HEAVEN AND *earth to witness against you today; I place before you life and death, blessing and curse. Choose life, so that you and your children will live*" (Deut 30:19-20). In this verse, God clearly points out the reality of blessing and curse. Each will be present every day and we must choose between the two. Blessings are always life-giving and curses always life-diminishing. When we choose blessings, the Lord tells us that we are choosing life, not only for ourselves but for our loved ones.

In the Old Testament, the Hebrew word for bless is *barak*. It literally means "God's intentions." Blessing opens a door to the goodness of God, to all that God intends for our lives. Some would describe blessing as God's favor poured out upon us, upon the person being blessed and even upon the blesser. When we bless a friend or family member, or even that ornery next-door neighbor, we are praying for all the goodness that God desires for that individual to be released in their life. The focus of blessing prayers draws our eyes away from the present need or situation and onto God's intention and desire for each individual and situation.

According to Scripture, God's intention is fullness of life for us and our family (Deut 30:19-20 and John 10:10b).

Words spoken and decisions made that align with the heart of God are all blessings, releasing God's love and mercy and healing light into the world. When you and I choose to bless, we are empowered and led by the Holy Spirit to be partners in ministry with Jesus. It is so important that we realize that God's blessing ministry is part of Jesus' resurrection ministry because blessings are always life-giving. Blessings replace fear with love. Blessings substitute judgmental, negative thinking and action with God's intended purpose. *The power of blessing bridges the chasm of polarization and division that separate us, God's people, from one another.* It gives us the opportunity to listen and actually hear the voice of both friend and foe, of ally and enemy. These are moments where our tightly held perceptions and opinions can begin to shift for the person speaking the words of blessing and the one receiving the blessing. Where we begin to see one another as God sees us. What an amazing life-transforming gift! This is the power of blessing that Jesus brings into the world, yesterday, today and for all the days to come. Friends, choose life—choose the way of blessing that you and your children will live.

The Power of Curse

For many Christians, "curse" is a misunderstood word. It tends not to be part of our religious vocabulary. Most of us have had little teaching on what a curse is. Thus, we are left without knowing how curses impact our lives. What does the author of Deuteronomy want us to understand about curse when he writes, *"I place before you life and death, blessing and curse"*? I believe he is not talking about swearing or using those four-letter words that often appear in our thoughts and on our lips when provoked or angered. A curse has a deeper, life altering meaning.

The author of Deuteronomy says blessing and curse are compared to life and death. Blessings bring life. Curses result in death. Blessings open us to the heart of God where life is to be received and experienced in all its God-given glory, in all its full-ness. Curses cast a life-diminishing shadow, usually upon a certain area of our life. When cursing becomes habitual for us, that shadow can and will begin to spread into other areas of our lives, resulting in a life focused on ourselves and filled with loneliness, sadness and fear. Jesus describes it like this: *"The thief comes only to steal and kill and destroy. I have come that they may have life, and have it to the full"* (John 10:10).

Satan is that thief. He comes to steal our peace and joy. He works to rob us of our blessings. He is the world's "Professor of Curses," highly gifted and skilled at his craft of cursing one another, and he will do almost anything to get us to enroll in his Cursing 101 class. He's been doing it for centuries, which explains in part why it is so challenging for us to move out from underneath Satan's influence of cursing one another. The reality is that Satan is having a field day due to our ignorance or resistance or simply "I'm not interested in this topic (this part of my life)." This results in our being even more vulnerable to the influence of curses.

So much of the deepening polarization and division happening in our society today is a result of the subtle and not so subtle curses we speak and decisions we make that run counter to what God intends for us. For the most part, we (the church) have fallen asleep when it comes to the power of blessing and curse. It is time for us to arise from our slumber. Jesus is saying, *"Wake up, sleeper, rise from the dead, and Christ will shine on you"* (Eph 5:14). The Good News is that the light of Christ always vanquishes the darkness of curse through our Holy Spirit empowered blessings spoken in Jesus' name.

The Human Tendency to Curse

The Power of Blessing by Kerry Kirkwood is one of the most insightful books I have recently read on the human tendency to curse. His writings helped expand my understanding of blessing ministry. In particular, I became aware of the subtle ways where we (I) are prone to see someone in a lesser way than God sees them. This is how Kirkwood defines a curse. It happens frequently through our thoughts, words and actions.

Just the other day I was driving home from running errands. The roads were crowded and very busy. I glanced in my rearview mirror and caught a glimpse of a small sports car speeding up behind me. That car suddenly veered over into the left lane to pass me, barely missing my back fender. Thoughts such as "What an idiot" and "That guy is going to get someone killed." There it is. There is the curse, words of anger spoken and thrown like a dart towards the driver of that car. Regardless of the danger he puts himself and others in through his unsafe driving, my thoughts and perspective of this person were so much less than God's thoughts and perspective about him. Do you see how subtle this is? I realized that I have a tendency to curse others, especially when I'm out driving. Someone riding my back bumper, especially out on the open road drives me crazy and a few choice words are on my lips without thinking about it. I'm late for a meeting and I get caught behind someone driving thirty miles per hour in a forty-five mile-per-hour zone. Yep, here come those words again.

For some time, I have felt an awareness that such words were demeaning and unkind. But I couldn't name it. I couldn't see that my thoughts and words placed the other person in a position far less than God holds them. Through Pastor Kirkwoods' book, the Lord helped me to understand that I have a human tendency of cursing others when someone does or says something that I find irritating. I began to understand that my tendency to be judgmental and critical of others can so easily turn into a word curse once I give those tendencies a voice. And it only takes a word or two. As James says, *"From the same mouth come blessing and cursing. My brothers and sisters, this ought not to be so"* (Jas 3:10).

What about you? Are there areas in your life where the words or actions of others trigger words of anger, judgement, and criticism within you? I believe the answer is probably yes for most of us. If it is true for you, I encourage you to ask Jesus if there are times when you have participated in the human tendency of cursing. Ask the Lord to point out examples where you are most prone to not choosing life for yourself and another person. It is so subtle isn't it? Who would even begin to think that such words could be a curse. I didn't, but I do now.

Where Cursing Enters

> Now the serpent was more crafty [subtle] than any of the wild animals the Lord God had made. He said to the woman, "Did God really say, 'You must not eat from any tree in the garden'?"
>
> The woman said to the serpent, "We may eat fruit from the trees in the garden, but God did say, 'You must not eat fruit from the tree that is in the middle of the garden, and you must not touch it, or you will die,'"
>
> "You will certainly not die," the serpent said to the woman. "For God knows that when you eat from it your eyes will be opened, and you will be like God, knowing good and evil."

(Gen 3:1–4)

In this short dialogue, Satan presents a choice to Eve and Adam. To eat or not to eat *from the tree of the knowledge of good and evil* (Gen 3:17). They probably didn't realize it at that moment, but the choice given them was blessing or curse. Obedience or disobedience to God. According to Scripture, obedience and blessing are intimately linked. *"All these blessings will come on you and accompany you if you obey the Lord your God"* (Deut 28:2). Similarly, disobedience and curses are closely tied together. *"However, if you do not obey the Lord your God and do not carefully follow all his commands and decrees I am giving you today, all these curses will come on you and overtake you"* (Deut 28:15).

The story of Adam and Eve reveals the source of our human tendency to curse—Satan. It also reveals when God's paradise on earth, the Garden of Eden, became infected with cursing, when Adam and Eve disobeyed God. Little has changed over the centuries. Whenever we are disobedient to God's will, I believe we have chosen curse over blessing. Whether we realize it or not, this is a moment when we have fallen prey to the wily and subtle ways of the evil one. It is so important that we understand that a curse casts a life-diminishing shadow over both the one doing the cursing and the one being cursed. The consequences can be dire and immediately felt. The shadow of a curse can be far-reaching. For example, cursing is always accompanied by decreased joy and peace in our lives. Just think about those times when you were upset with someone and said things out of anger or judgment. Can you recall ever feeling at peace or overflowing with joy at such times? No, of course not.

Remember the story of Carolyn mentioned in Chapter 3? Though she repeatedly tried to forgive, she was unable to let go of her unforgiveness. Why? Her focus kept returning to the hurt and resentment caused by her son and daughter-in-laws' behavior. Anger, fear, unforgiveness, bitterness are all associated with curse. For two years the power of cursing held her captive. As soon as she began to speak blessing prayers over her son and daughter-in-law, Carolyn, experienced immediate healing and freedom for herself. The power of blessings can free us from our wounded past by simply speaking God's intentions, God's love, God's purpose over those who have hurt us. Cursing closes the door to the nature of God in our lives. Blessings open the door, drawing us deeper into the heart of God.

Love Your Enemies

"You have heard that it was said, 'You shall love your neighbor and hate your enemy.' But I say to you, love your enemies, bless those who curse you, do good to those who hate you, and pray for those who spitefully use you and persecute you" (Matt 5:43–44). Clearly Jesus is calling us to change our ways in how we respond to our enemies, to those who curse us. Those who speak and act poorly towards us. Those who spread gossip and rumors about us. Those who believe such gossip and rumors.

When I read or hear Jesus say, *love your enemy*, my humanity rears up and says, "No." My longtime, trusted friend just betrayed me at work by spreading lies about something I never did. "Love him? Love her, after what she did, what he said?" My humanity literally wants to shout, "No way am I going to love my enemy." This is part of our dilemma as followers of Jesus. Set before us every day is blessing and curse. We are called to choose life, to be a people of blessing. Jesus says love those who curse you, betray you, speak falsely about you or about a loved one. How do we love such individuals? *Jesus tells us how! "Bless those who curse you."* Though I am still susceptible to "DUIs," that is, driving (living) under the influence of cursing, I am making noticeable progress in blessing those who use to anger or irritate me. It began with a choice, a choice to bless rather than curse. I found myself beginning to speak words of blessing.

In Jesus' name, I bless [name/names] with God's love flowing directly from Abba's heart into his/her heart. I bless [name/names] with a fresh in-filling of the Holy Spirit that brings Godly wisdom and truth into all areas of his/her life, including their decision-making. I bless [name/names] with the fullness of God's intentions for his/her life. And in Jesus' name, I speak these words of blessing over my family and myself as well. I bless us all with coming home to our true self in Christ. Amen.

It is a choice that confronts us all . . . to live a life of cursing (hating your enemy) or to live a life of blessing (loving your enemies.) The following story describes the challenge of making the choice to bless.

Pastor Tim had to drive by the newly opened adult entertainment business on the way to and from his church. For several weeks he prayed every time he drove by yet saw no change. Out of frustration he switched from praying to speaking curses over the establishment. The owner of the bar had become his enemy. The shadow of Tim's curses spread out to include each employee and every patron. The more Tim cursed the more cars filled their parking lot. Pastor Tim felt helpless and didn't know what to do. A few days went by and Jesus intervened with these words, *"Tim, stop cursing my people. I died on the cross for them as much as I did for you! Your curses only serve to strengthen Satan's hold on them and brings you under his influence as well."* When asked what to do, Jesus instructed him to start blessing his enemy.

When I first read this story, I could almost hear God saying to Tim, "Speak words of my love and mercy, blessings that I intend to pour out upon them. Your words of blessing will release a river of living water flowing from my throne room into the lives of owner, employees, and patrons alike. The doors to this darkness will be closed and the way back into my heart will be revealed to them. Bless my people in Jesus' name and you will see my light vanquish darkness, my love cast out fear, and my joy replace your worries and concerns." Pastor Tim began to bless and lives were changed, just as the Lord said it would. By the way, the business closed its doors within weeks of when Tim began to love his enemies through blessing prayers. Such is the power of blessing!

Remember, blessings spoken in Jesus' name has the power to bridge the gap between ourselves and those we have a conflicted or estranged relationship. What "enemy" is Jesus calling you to bless? A politician? A co-worker? A family member? A neighbor? A pastor? It is a choice that confronts us all at some point . . . .to live a life of cursing (hating your enemy) during times of deep stress and anger or to live a life of blessing those who curse you (loving your enemy) as Jesus instructs. Part of the Good News is that Jesus always sends the Holy Spirit to help us with words of blessing to speak, to pray once we choose the way of blessing. We are never alone in blessing others. Jesus is always with us as we seek to be obedient to his words, *"Love your enemies."*

Questions for Reflection and Study

1. What are some of the significant characteristics of the power of blessing?

2. Would you agree that we all have a human tendency to curse others with our words and actions? Examples of when you have fallen into the trap of cursing others by word or deed?

3. Are there moments or places in your life where you need God's help to begin speaking words that bless rather than curse?

7

Healing and Reconciling Relationships

RIGHT ABOUT NOW, I want to shout out words of praise and thanksgiving to God. Through the death and resurrection of Jesus new life is given to all. The stone to Jesus' tomb is rolled away. The door to God's heart has been flung wide open. The power of the Holy Spirit at work in Jesus' resurrection is calling all his daughters and sons back home to the Father. Our words and acts of blessing open the door to the heart of God, for both ourselves (our inherited blessing) and to those we bless.

"*Therefore, if anyone is in Christ, the new creation has come: The old has gone, the new is here*" (2 Cor 5:17). Part of the old is our tendency to curse. The new is blessing in Jesus' name. Thus, "*from now on we regard no one from a worldly point of view*" (2 Cor 5:16). Jesus frees us from the curse of viewing and treating others in lesser ways than God does. We are free from this worldly way of viewing one another (and all of creation for that matter). The Holy Spirit gives us new eyes, where we can see one another as God sees us. Beloved. Valued. Cherished. Forgiven. Redeemed. Healed. Reconciled!

We are now stepping into what may be the heart of blessing prayer—the ministry of reconciliation. On the cross, Jesus' spoke these unimaginable words of blessing, *"Father, forgive them, for they do not know what they are doing"* (Luke 23:34). Through these words, Jesus began reconciling all of humankind back to God the Father. In Jesus' suffering on the cross, the heart of the Father had never been so wide open, so vulnerable and so unconditionally loving than at this moment. Here, blessing and reconciliation merge into a new oneness, a unity of Spirit seeking to reconcile all of creation with God our Creator.

Jesus so often taught and prayed for healing and reconciliation amongst the people, no matter if they were Jews or gentiles, believers or non-believers. The story of Jesus' encounter with a group of Pharisees reveals how central healing and reconciliation are to Jesus' primary mission. *"When the Pharisees heard that he [Jesus] had silenced the Sadducees, they gathered together, and one of them, a lawyer, asked him a question to test him. 'Teacher, which commandment in the law is the greatest?' He said to him, 'You shall love the Lord your God with all your heart, and with all your soul, and with all your mind.' This is the greatest and first commandment. And a second is like it: You shall love your neighbor as yourself.' On these two commandments hang all the law and prophets'"* (Matt 22: 34-40).

Everything hinges on our choosing to love God and to love our neighbor. According to Jesus, we cannot do one without the other being greatly affected. To love God means we must also love our neighbor. To do one without the other means we have fallen short of keeping both commandments. I believe that loving God with our whole heart, soul and mind compels us to love our neighbor. If we are not loving our neighbor as ourselves, then we are not fully keeping the commandment of loving God with our entire being. These two commandments are that intimately intertwined.

Unfortunately, there are ornery neighbors and bullies in the world. Probably every neighborhood has one or two. When I think about a few of my past neighbors, it is not love that comes to mind. Rather, a few memories arise of misunderstandings leading to angry words and withdrawing from one another. I want to be clear that you understand it was not just my neighbor who spoke angry words and withdrew from me. There were times when I acted the same. Who of us haven't had similar experiences? Who of us haven't been challenged to love our neighbors as Jesus instructs? It can be one of the most challenging and uncomfortable tasks that we ever face. What can we do?

God has given us a way to love all our neighbors. It is the way of blessing. No matter if your neighbor is friend or adversary, we can love them through our words of blessing, such as:

> In Jesus' name, I bless (name) and myself with God's love flowing directly from Abba's heart into our hearts, casting out all fear. I bless (name) and myself with Jesus' peace, saturating our entire being, washing away all anger and worries. I bless (name) and myself with a fresh in-filling of the Holy Spirit that brings us more and more of God's truth and understanding into our relationship; that renews and heals (name) wherever needed; that draws each of us closer to Jesus. I bless (name) and myself with coming home to our true self. In Jesus' name I pray. Amen.

The way of blessing includes speaking the same blessings over my neighbor as I would myself. This is why I included the word *myself* in the blessing prayer you just read. It frees us to love our neighbor without animosity and all the human emotions involved. It begins with a choice to follow God's commandments to love, both God and neighbor. It continues with listening to the Holy Spirit for words of blessing that God would have us speak. It includes listening for blessings to speak that our heart desires for this person and for ourselves. Then we simply begin praying blessings in Jesus' name. This opens the door to healing and reconciliation between my neighbor and myself.

Paul says, *"All this is from God, who reconciled us to himself through Christ and gave us the ministry of reconciliation"* (2 Cor 5:18). The very fact that the power of blessing can so easily overcome the power of cursing provides new possibilities for reconciliation. As I listen to the evening news and to conversations at my favorite local diner, I hear so many stories of how differences in our worldview, whether it be political, cultural or theological, are separating us more and more into camps of "like mindedness." The resulting isolation seems to only heighten our human tendency towards judgmental and critical thoughts of others, making us easy prey in succumbing to the way of cursing, of seeing and treating one another so much less than God does. The need for blessing ministry is rising significantly throughout the world. We are being called to bless and to restore God's ministry of blessing. As we do so, we will begin to see our shared humanity through God's eyes. We will begin to see anew that we are brothers and sisters in Christ, each of us beloved and cherished and valued by God. The power of blessing will bridge the gap that separate us, drawing us to a place of healing and reconciliation.

The following story was shared with me a few years ago during a healing conference. It is a story of healing and reconciliation between a mother and daughter.

Healing and Reconciling a Relationship
(mother and daughter)

John, the last time you were here, you taught us about blessing prayers. You had us practice speaking blessing prayers with one another. It was a wonderful experience for me.

When I arrived home, I felt the Holy Spirit nudging me to begin speaking blessing prayers over my daughter. About a year ago, she and I had a terrible argument. Fueled by anger, each of us spoke words that we never would have said to one another. We have not spoken nor seen each other since. I know my angry words hurt her deeply. Her words did the same to me. I prayed and prayed. My prayers weren't working.

Then I heard you talking about blessing ministry and God's promise to release his goodness and grace whenever we bless one another in Jesus' name. I realized that I was being given a new way to pray for my daughter and our relationship. I decided to start speaking blessings over her every day, beginning that very evening. Within a few weeks, my daughter called! Words of forgiveness were spoken and received. My relationship with my daughter is closer and stronger than ever, and so is my relationship with Jesus.

Anonymous

God promises to release more of his goodness, grace, and love whenever we speak blessings over one another. This brings new possibilities for healing and reconciliation, especially where relationships have been damaged or broken. The following is a powerful blessing story of healing and reconciliation between a dying man and Jesus.

Healing Relationship with Jesus

My father-in-law, Bill Sr., lay on his death bed. We were told that he had 4-8 days to live. My husband, Bill, and his sister Anne, went out to get some lunch, and I was left alone with Bill Sr.

Now Bill Sr. had Alzheimer's so badly that he had not recognized anyone or spoken a complete sentence in months. His brain was gone; as my husband would say, "Dad has left the building!" Also, Bill Sr. had struggled with doubt about faith in God for as long as I had known him. He had a hard time believing that there could be a good God when there was so much suffering and pain in the world. *And as a physician, he had seen a lot of suffering.*

As I sat in the chair, observing him and asking the Lord to show me what to do, I felt the Holy Spirit move me to lean over on the bed and get very close to Bill's face. I took his hand in mine, and I started to bless his spirit. I said, "Bill, I bless your spirit, in the name of Jesus, to know that God knows you by name and you are His! I bless you to know that you are fearfully and wonderfully made by God and He loves you! I bless you to know that He says, "Well done, good and faithful servant!" I bless you to know that Jesus has gone to prepare a place for you; if it were not so, He would have told us. You are safe and you are loved. Your doubts are not too big for God. He welcomes all of who you are into all of who He is. Trust Him. He will never leave you or forsake you."

And when I took a breath, Bill Sr. squeezed my hand! I was shocked! His spirit was hearing and understanding my words, even though his brain was so impaired!

So, I started reciting every scripture that I could remember, and he would occasionally lift his ear off of the pillow to hear me better! He continued to occasionally squeeze my hand in response to the scripture that I was saying. I sang every hymn I could remember. Tears were streaming down my face. The Holy Spirit was filling me with God's love for Bill Sr. And Bill Sr. said "Yes!" to that love by squeezing my hand!

When Bill and Anne returned, I told them, "Your Father will be in Heaven when he dies. I have NO DOUBT that he has said "Yes!" to Jesus today, no matter what his struggles were in his earthly life." To hear those words was such a joy to Bill and his sister.

The rest of the day, Bill and Anne kept the vigil. After dinner, Bill prayed, "Dad I bless your spirit to rise when the sun rises tomorrow." And that is exactly what happened. Before we could get to the bedside the next day, the nurses called us to say: "We are so sorry: we had no idea he was going to pass away today! We were in the room with him, and he was stable. We went out to order medication, and when we came back in, he was gone!"

Bill said, "Oh don't be sorry! God heard my prayer and so did my dad's spirit! His spirit rose with the sun!" And we all rejoiced: the battle was over and the victory was won!

Katie (North Carolina)

Katie's powerful blessing story is a story of God's love (God's blessings!) being released upon Bill Sr. through his son and daughter-in-law. It is a story that reveals this truth: wherever God's love dwells there will always be possibilities of healing and reconciliation. Their story reminds us that in God's love there is no such thing as, "Bill, you're too late" or "Sorry, Bill, but you missed your chance." Paul puts it this way, *"For I am sure that neither death, nor life, nor angels, nor principalities, nor things to come, nor powers, nor height, nor depth, nor anything else in all creation, will be able to separate us from the love of God in Christ Jesus our Lord"* (Rom 8: 38-39) AMEN!

Questions for Reflection and Study

1. Have you ever found yourself saying no to loving your neighbor as yourself? What might Jesus say to you about those times? Take a moment to pray, to listen to what he wants to share with you.

2. Do you have a neighbor, either next door or at work or at church, that you find difficult to love? Ask Jesus to help you begin to speak blessing prayers over that person(s) as well for yourself.

3. Are there relationships where healing is meant to happen but not necessarily reconciliation? What are examples of where this might be true?

8

Healing and Reconciling God's Creation Through Blessings

Throughout this book, I have turned to Scripture, to the knowledge and life experiences of several friends and to authors regarding blessing ministry. This next section is co-authored by my wife. This is the result of our conversations about creation and how blessings and curses impact God's very gift of creation.

Debra

"In the beginning"—God calls creation good. The word "good" is both an adjective and a verb. In the act of calling something good, God (and we) actually bless it. We bless it by confirming and affirming its true nature. In Genesis, God blesses all parts of nature over and over again. And then, God makes humans "in his image." To be made in God's image means to share in the work, to do as our Father did and does. And what is that work? Blessing.

John

In the story of creation, as recorded in the book of Genesis, God looks upon what he has created and says, " . . . *it was good!*" Six times, God gazes upon what he has just created and each time God says, "*. . . it was good,*" except for the seventh time. "*And God saw every thing that he had made, and, behold, it was very good.*" (Gen 1: 31) God is so pleased with his creation. I can just imagine God saying, 'This creation is filled with my beauty and majesty and splendor. It will sustain my people over the ages and reflect my glory to all the inhabitants. All they have to do is take care of it as I would.' We are caretakers of creation—caring for God's creation through continued words and acts of blessing, releasing God's goodness upon and into what he has created.

Debra

Blessing creation is essentially the first work that God gives us. But what about the "dominion" part (Gen 1:26)? (Here the word "dominion" is a more accurate translation than using the word subdue.) To be granted dominion has several layers of meaning, typical of the rich Hebrew Scripture. Dominion can have lordly, kingly connotations. But we need to look at that with Hebrew eyes. In that time and in that place, a king had only two jobs: (1) Be utterly faithful to God's gift of covenant and (2) protect all of God's gifts. Yes, even to keep creation safe. It is no surprise that in many psalms, a king is referred to as shepherd—one who keeps and protects.

Dominion can also mean "to be a steward" . . . to be the onsite caretaker when the true owner is busy with other work. "To be a steward" means to care for something as the owner intends. We are God's hands and feet and muscle on this earth and we must care for it as such. When God called creation "good," he did not say, "pretty good, needs some work here, a little fixing there." He said, "good." In the beginning, the earth needed no fixing. But now it does because humans (we) have broken it, rather than blessing it.

John

God instructs Adam (Gen 2:15) "to till and keep the land [Garden of Eden]" . . . .to farm the land and to take care of it. To till and to keep are the first works of blessings assigned to Adam and Eve, to humanity. To till means to "work" the soil, preparing the soil (the work of blessing), readying it to be planted with seed and crop. To keep the land (garden) has to do with caring for it, specifically calling us to protect the land. The Garden of Eden was Adam and Eve's, original home and God specifically instructs them to protect their land. But what would they have to protect the Garden (the land) from? After all, they are living in a God created paradise.

The answer comes from the story of Adam and Eve in their encounter with the serpent recorded in Gen 3:1–4. The serpent approaches the couple and starts the conversation with this familiar question, *"Did God say, 'You must not eat from any tree in the garden?'"* Most know the rest of the story. But something seems amiss. What is the serpent (Satan) doing in the Garden? Remember, Satan, also known as Lucifer, was kicked out of heaven along with thousands of other angels that joined him in his rebellion against God. Doesn't it feel really strange that he would be in the Garden of Eden?

However, neither Adam nor Eve seems to be surprised at his presence. They don't appear to be startled at all. Rather, Eve engages him in conversation as if it was normal. Here lies the answer to the question, "What does Adam and Eve need to protect the Garden from?" It is Satan. The Father of lies. The author of curses. The source of all brokenness.

The fall or breakup between God and Adam and Eve continues today. We have strayed. Too often we have not been obedient to God's instructions to bless the land. We have not sought the fullness of God's intentions for the land and for each other. We have given into the human tendency to replace blessing with curses. How? By choosing neglect over caretaking, "mining" the soil for all it has to give with little regard to replenishment and sustainability. The air and waterways have too often been treated as dumping sites for pollutants of all sorts, resulting in diminished health and well-being of God's creation. As Deb said, the earth is broken. We have broken it, rather than blessed it.

The good news is that we have the capability, the wisdom and knowledge, to mend what is broken. We can do this by following God's instructions to be good stewards of God's creation, keeping and protecting our "island home." Stewarding of the earth is meant to enhance and sustain the fullness of God's intentions for both the land and for God's people . . . .for all of God's creation. For example, from an agricultural point of view, it is never an either-or choice. I believe that God never meant us to choose between "tilling the land" (for food production and profit) or "keeping the land" (for long term soil vitality and sustainability). God says do both. "Keeping (protecting) the land" ensures high crop yields over the centuries. "Tilling the land" produces those yields on a yearly basis.

Debra

Over and over, the prophets (at least Isaiah, Jeremiah and most of the "minor" prophets) detail how humanity's penchant for cursing has led to tragedy. This tragedy is even felt by God's very creation. Hosea says it plainly for ears then and now.

> *Hear the word of the Lord, O people of Israel; for the Lord has an indictment against the inhabitants of the land. There is no faithfulness or loyalty, and no knowledge of God in the land.*
>
> *Swearing, lying, and murder, and stealing and adultery break out; bloodshed follows bloodshed.*
>
> *Therefore the land mourns, and all who live in it languish; together with the wild animals and the birds of the air, even the fish of the sea are perishing.* (Hos 4:1-3)

It is the last phrase of verse 1 that broke my heart open. "*There is no faithfulness or loyalty, and no knowledge of God in the land.*" Remembering that Hebrew text usually has multiple layers of meaning: what if "God in the land" means not simply "neighborhood," but God *in* the land? God's light/life is present *in* the soil, landscape, water—all the created physical components of that neighborhood. To live a life of cursing and covenant-breaking (the swearing, lying, etc.) leads to not just humans hurting but the very land hurting. The cry of humans hurt by cursing is joined by the literal cry of the land, wild animals, birds, and even sea creatures! And this mournful cry is even more insistent when we make sad excuses for abusing God's gift of creation.

From the beginning of creation, God asks us to keep covenant with him. A covenant is a promise of partnership between two parties. In the Hebrew Testament that means God and God's children—us. The giver of the gift of covenant (God) cannot break covenant. But the recipient (humankind) of that gift can and does break it over and over. In the Hebrew Testament, multiple covenants are made and broken. Each of those covenants is made with different "main characters" during different times in Hebrew history. While details may vary, two truths are common to the covenant stories: (1) God's people have broken their promises to love and care for what/whom God loves. (2) God's people have broken their promises to have "no other god's before me" (Exod 20:3, Deut 5:7). In spite of this, God repeatedly says I want to restore our relationship. Will you honor and love as a sign? Will you bless as I bless? Will your actions embody that blessing?

I think that humanity's cursing—in word and deed—has negated, or at least diminished the blessing of creation. Just as our human bodies remember abuse, so does the "body" of the earth. As Hosea knew, our abuse, misuse, carelessness, greed and unconscious disregard has led to rampant degradation of our environment. Cursing has consequences. Those consequences can extend like vast crabgrass roots to overpower the beautiful blessing of creation.

John

Where do we start in healing the land? In reconciling God's creation with God's people? Blessing the land is a powerful starting place. We can speak blessing prayers over the land and over those whose vocations are directly tied to keeping and tilling the land. We all have a role to play in healing and reconciling our neighborhood portion of God's creation. God calls us to choose life. Jesus calls us to be a people of blessing as a way of choosing life, of healing and reconciling God's creation with the Creator and with one another.

Questions for Reflection and Study

1. In what ways have you personally cursed/abused God's gift of creation?

2. How can you actively bless God's creation? How can you bless with words? How can you bless with action? How can you bless with your life?

3. What statement in this chapter most "breaks open your heart"? Why?

4. What statement in this chapter gives you the most hope? Why?

9

Ministry Guidelines

THIS CHAPTER IS MEANT to provide basic guidelines in speaking blessing prayers. As with any new practice, there is usually a learning curve involved. The difference between praying words of blessing and praying our heart's desire for another person is significant. Both ways of praying are needed. I'm certain that God hears our heart's cry and our words of blessing because we pray both in Jesus' name. To suddenly switch to praying blessing prayers often needs a period of practice, of putting your hearts desire into words of blessing. The Holy Spirit will teach and lead you. The more you speak blessing prayers, the more natural it will become. This has been my experience and the experience of many others.

The following guidelines are not a formula for every situation and need. They are meant to serve as an outline for blessing ministry. The Holy Spirit will provide the words of blessing to speak for each blessing prayer opportunity God gives you.

1. The heart of blessing ministry

God calls us to be a people of blessing. It's a profound and life changing call to discipleship and ministry. Seeking God's intention and desire and purpose for our lives lies at the heart of blessing ministry.

Our lives will be transformed, freeing us to love and be loved as Jesus loves us; to experience Jesus' overflowing peace and joy, every day. Blessings open us to receiving and sharing the fullness of abundant life that Jesus deeply desires to give us—a life characterized by freedom from the darkness of sin and the lies and deceptions of the Evil One. It is a life filled with love given and received, a life filled with blessings shared and inherited.

2. Called to bless often involves a change of heart.

Early in my blessing ministry journey, my focus was on learning as much about God's ministry of blessing as I could. Initially God provided many opportunities for me to speak (practice!) blessings prayers. My excitement increased as I witnessed God fulfilling his promise to release blessings when we, The Blessing Place Ministry Team, spoke words of blessing in Jesus' name. Gradually, I began to see a deeper change that was happening, one that was happening within me.

I realized that I needed more of God's goodness and grace released in my life as much as anyone else. In this way, blessing ministry becomes a great equalizer for the people of God. You and I are called to bless others and at the same time, we stand in need of God's continued blessings as well. I am so thankful that I am called to bless and to teach others in becoming a people of blessing. But in no way does this mean that I need God's goodness and mercy any less than those I am called to bless. Accepting this truth about ourselves is a key to effective blessing ministry.

3. Choose the Way of Blessing every day (1 Pet 3:9).

While talking about blessing Peter wrote, *"It is for this you were called."* God's Word describes our discipleship as a way of blessing, to be a people looking for opportunities to speak blessing prayers every day. We can bless the ill and suffering. We can bless our family members. We can bless neighbors and colleagues, local businesses and farmers. We can bless our churches and ministries, schools, students and staff. We can bless local, state and national leaders . . . all in Jesus' name!

God's design for his ministry of blessing is perfect. We are all uniquely created by God. This means that your "yes" to blessing ministry will have its very own unique sound and expression. *No one can express blessing prayers as you can and there is no other person who can live out the Way of Blessing as God has created you to do.* You are needed. We are all needed in restoring God's ministry of blessing.

4. Always bless in Jesus' Name (Num 6:27).

God's only condition attached to his promise to bless is to speak the words of blessing in his name. This is why we always speak blessing prayers in Jesus' name. The goodness and grace God releases when we speak blessings in Jesus' name are filled with the living hope and resurrection power of Jesus himself.

5. Ask the Holy Spirit to lead you (John 16:13).

The leading of the Holy Spirit in speaking blessings is two-fold. Pray for the Holy Spirit to give you discernment if you are to speak blessings over an individual, a situation . . . or not. If yes, pray for the Holy Spirit to give you specific words of blessings to share. The Holy Spirit desires to do both in blessing ministry. It is all part of God's design.

Be encouraged. We are never alone in blessing ministry. God is always with us through the indwelling presence and power of his Holy Spirit.

6. Speak words of blessings out loud.

God knows our thoughts and hears our words. Speaking words of blessing out loud or silently as a thought are both effective ways to bless. Yet, there seems to be something extra, something more to blessing prayers when spoken out loud. Perhaps it is something as simple as realizing that we cannot speak without breathing. It is part of how we are created. Go ahead and try to speak a few words without exhaling. It can't be done. Air has to pass over our vocal cords in order for words to be uttered. I think something similar happens with blessing prayers to be most effective. Breathe in the Holy Spirit and exhale God's love though words of blessings! Speak blessings out loud whenever possible.

7. Blessing prayers can be said one on one and corporately.

There is considerable flexibility in speaking blessing prayers. Blessing prayers can be spoken one on one as well as for a group of people with similar effectiveness. The stories in this book repeatedly reveal this truth.

8. The person (group) being blessed does not have to be present.

A commonly asked question: Does the person/group being blessed have to be present for our blessing prayers to be effective? It is a good question and can be answered simply and with certainty. God's promise to release blessings is dependent upon one condition only, blessing in Jesus' name. Individuals being blessed do not have to be physically present nor even be aware that others are speaking blessings over them.

9. Blessing prayers are a powerful healing prayer.

The stories of Ed, Carolyn, Alice, Bill Sr. and others reveal the healing power God releases through our blessing prayers. I have highlighted the healing of relationships in several of these stories. Most recently, the Holy Spirit has been teaching us ways of blending blessing prayers with other healing prayer methods (see chapter 11 and 12) resulting in the fullness of God's wellness and wholeness that God desires for us.

10. Speak blessings for a specific outcome.

Praying for God's will to be done in a person's life, especially in a particular area of need, is always an appropriate prayer. At the same time, God already knows our heart's desire for this person. Blessing prayers provide a way for us to be completely open to God with those desires, including specific outcomes. For example, where relationships are estranged, we speak words of blessing for healing and reconciliation. In a financially struggling business, God knows our hearts, so go ahead and speak words of blessing for financial prosperity. For a college graduate, words of blessing for just the right job that provides good income and a healthy work environment can have great impact. For a farming community, be free to speak words of blessing for bountiful crops and livestock, adequate labor, and for family health and well-being.

11. The freedom to pray without an agenda.

In our humanity, there are times when our frustrations with others tend to leak into our prayer life. We tell ourselves that we know exactly what they need and then share that with God as we pray for them. Who of us have not prayed this way or at least been tempted to pray like this? Blessing prayers provide a way to let go of our human agenda, freeing us from frustrations and other highly charged feelings and freeing us from our own biases and prejudices. We are freed to pray with Spirit-desired outcomes.

Example: that political leader who makes you wonder, "How can they even think that?" or "How can they be so blind to the consequences their vote will have upon others (the environment, local businesses, refugees, etc.)?" Blessing prayers provides a "new way" to pray, setting us free to pray without personal bias or judgement. For political leaders, whether local, state or national, I now pray like this, *"In Jesus' name, I bless (political name) with a fresh infilling of the Holy Spirit, awakening them to the Spirit's truth and wisdom and to justice and compassion for God's people in all their deliberations. I bless them with Abba's love flowing directly from God's heart into their heart. I bless them with the light and love of Christ shining upon them and all those they love, protecting them both night and day. In Jesus' name I pray. Amen."* Notice that this blessing prayer can be used very effectively for leaders whose views are similar to yours as well as those whose views are polar opposite of yours. Speaking words of blessing carries an expectation and understanding that God desires to release his goodness and grace as God knows will be best for this person, this group of people and for ourselves.

12. There is no partiality in God's ministry of blessing.

In most liturgical churches, Sunday worship services usually conclude with the pastor speaking a blessing over the congregation. The concluding or "sending forth" blessing I often said was, *"The peace of God that passes all understanding keep your heart and mind in the knowledge and love of God and of his son, Jesus Christ our Lord. And the blessing of God almighty, Father, Son, and Holy Spirit be upon you and those you love this day and forever more."* During my last few years of parish ministry, I sensed the Spirit's leading to add these important words, " . . . . And the blessing of God almighty, Father, Son, and Holy Spirit be upon you, those you love *and those that you do not* this day and forever more!"

These additional words of blessing invariably elicited chuckles amongst the congregation. It always felt like a very human response to hearing God's truth spoken, realizing that we have not always embraced that truth in our own lives. I am so thankful for this Holy Spirit edit to my "sending forth" blessing, as it reveals how God seeks to bless all of God's people! As written in Acts 10:34: *"Then Peter began to speak to them: 'I truly understand that God shows no partiality . . . '"* (NRSV). Another translation (Worldwide English) puts it this way: *"Then Peter began to speak, 'I really understand now. God does not love some people more than others . . . '"* God's ministry of blessing provides a way for us to pray without partiality. What an amazing gift this is, a way to pray without our human bias and prejudices getting in the way. This is what the Spirit does when our words of blessing are prayed in Jesus' name. Always.

13. Be persistent in your blessing prayers.

"One of Jesus' disciples said to him, *'Lord, teach us to pray, as John taught his disciples'*" (Luke 11:1).

Jesus responded to that prayer request by teaching them the Lord's Prayer. Then he told them a story about a friend who arrives late at night, probably unexpectedly as his host does not have enough food. The host goes to his neighbor at midnight to borrow three loaves of bread. The neighbor is reluctant to get up because all the family is asleep. Jesus says, *"I tell you, even though he will not get up and give him anything because he is his friend, at least because of his persistence he will get up and give him whatever he needs"* (Luke 11:8). Jesus instructs us to be persistent in our prayer life. Be persistent in speaking blessing prayers.

14. Pray blessing prayers for yourself as well as for others.

Most of us are usually much more skilled and comfortable in praying for others than in receiving prayer for ourselves. Blessing prayers can help overcome this imbalance. We can include ourselves when speaking words of blessing over others. Listen for the leading of the Holy Spirit of when to do this and when not to.

Family prayers are a good starting place to include yourself in blessing prayers. I use to bless my family like this. *"In Jesus' name, I bless my family [list names here] with love flowing directly from Abba's heart and my heart into their hearts. I bless my family with*

Jesus' peace and joy. I bless them with the discernment and wisdom of the Holy Spirit in all that they will encounter this day. I bless them with the Light of Christ to protect them from all harm of the Evil One." I would conclude my family blessing prayers with: "*I bless every member of my family in coming home to their true self, God's beloved daughters and sons. In Jesus' name I pray. Amen.*"

I eventually realized that I needed these blessings as much as my family did. So now I simply pray, "*In Jesus' name, I bless my family and myself*" or "*I bless us!*" Please don't neglect God's desire to pour out more of his goodness and grace upon you as you bless others. Listen for the Spirit's leading and be sure to include yourself in your blessing prayers when nudged by the Spirit. It is good for your health and your life!

15. What is loosed on earth is loosed in heaven.

What does Jesus mean when he tells his disciples, "*Whatever you bind on earth will be bound in heaven, and whatever you lose on earth will be loosed in heaven*" (Matt 16:19)? First, most of us would believe that God's actions are not dependent upon human action. Thank goodness for this. However, part of God's design for experiencing more freedom (loosening) and less captivity (binding) depends upon the choices we make. God gives us a choice and the consequences of our choices are experienced on earth and in heaven.

For example, when we choose to forgive someone, God's grace and forgiveness is loosed in heaven. I picture the flood gates of heaven opening so that God's grace and forgiveness rains down upon those we choose to forgive, and upon ourselves. When we choose to hold onto our unforgiveness towards another, then those same heavenly floodgates remain closed. I believe God's ministry of blessing works in a similar way.

Questions for Reflection and Study

Rather than providing questions for this chapter, I simply want to encourage you to go back and read each blessing ministry guideline slowly. Listen for what the Holy Spirit wants you to see, what else these guidelines can teach you.

10

Blending Blessing Prayers with Soaking Prayer

BLESSING PRAYERS ARE A powerful healing prayer all by themselves. Those experienced in healing prayer ministry already know that there is no one kind of prayer that works effectively in healing all emotional, spiritual and physical needs. I believe this is why the Holy Spirit began to show us how to blend blessing prayers with other kinds of healing prayers. Such blending of different kinds of healing prayer has been one of the most exciting and effective healing ministries that I have experienced. Here are a few examples of blending blessing prayers with other kinds of healing prayers.

Soaking Prayer

At a 2022 regional OSL Conference[1] in Wisconsin, I spoke on the basics of blessing prayer ministry. We then spent about thirty minutes praying for one another in small groups using blessing prayers. That is when I began to sense the Holy Spirit's leading for

---

1. The Order of St. Luke the Physician is an ecumenical Christian healing organization dedicated to restoring Jesus' healing ministry in the church.

us to use blessing prayers as part of our soaking prayer healing service that evening.

At its heart, soaking prayer is the blending of holy silence and Holy Spirit. It is a contemplative yet spirit-filled form of prayer. No words are spoken during the actual prayer time. This can be a wonderful gift to both the prayer recipient and prayer minister. For the prayer recipient, the silence seems to allow the Holy Spirit to take them deeper into the presence of God, the source of all healing and blessing. For the prayer minister, they simply become the conduit of the Holy Spirit at work within the prayer recipient. The silence frees the prayer minister from any sense of "having to say just the right words" or fear of "saying the wrong thing." The prayer minister continues to listen to the Holy Spirit and prays silently for each person's prayer request, written on a 3x5 card and made available to each prayer minister to read.

One of the ways to understand soaking prayer is to think about what happens during a time of extended drought when rain finally comes. When a drought continues in a region for a long period of time the soil becomes hard and starts to crack open. If a sudden storm passes through, with lots of rainfall in a short period of time, what happens to the rainwater? The soil is so dry and hard that most of the rain simply runs off. The soil surface may be damp, but the water cannot penetrate the soil to the plant roots where it is needed.

However, if a gentle soaking rain comes through, lasting for several hours, the soil can absorb the moisture. The rainwater penetrates to the plant roots where it can be taken up by the plant for restoration and growth. Something very similar happens during soaking prayer. The prayer recipient becomes saturated or "soaked" in the love of Jesus. Through the power of the Holy Spirit at work in the soaking prayer, Jesus' love and healing light gently penetrates into those dry broken places, bringing healing and restoration.

A close friend, Dr. Jim Sloan, referred to soaking prayer as marinating in God's presence. This is a great description of what occurs during soaking prayer ministry. When we marinate a steak for thirty minutes, the meat becomes tender and begins to pick up the flavor of the marinade. In soaking prayer, the marinade of God's love and peace begins to soften those dry hard places within us. Worries and fears are replaced with God's peace and love. Soaking prayer offers us the gift of *"taste and see that the Lord is good!"* (Ps 34:8), a gift that brings healing and restoration.

Here are a few additional notes about offering a soaking prayer healing service for your group or in your church. For a church healing service, we would try to schedule one prayer minister for every four people attending the service. The prayer ministers, musicians and I would meet for fifteen minutes prior to the service for a time of prayer and anointing for ourselves. Every other pew or row of chairs in the church sanctuary is roped off to give our prayer ministers room to move behind each person during soaking prayer time. Everyone attending the service would be given a copy of the liturgy (see Appendix) and a 3x5 card to write down their prayer requests (someone for whom they were already interceding and also a request specifically for themselves.) The soaking prayer ministry time comes at the end of the brief liturgy and lasts about thirty minutes.

The Wisconsin OSL Conference was the first time that I had ever asked the prayer ministers to specifically use blessing prayers during a soaking prayer healing service. The presence of the Holy Spirit was palpable. Afterwards, individuals shared what they had experienced. . . . *"relief from pain," "forgiveness for myself," "abiding peace replacing my worries and concerns," "discernment regarding an important decision," "the loving presence of Jesus."* We concluded the service with a time of giving God thanks and praise!

Questions for Reflection and Study

1. Are there elements of soaking prayer that you are drawn to? Which of these feels especially important to you?

2. How does soaking prayer differ from ways that you have been praying?

3. Which description of soaking prayer in this chapter was most helpful to you? Why?

11

Blending Blessing Prayers with Prayers for Physical Healing

In chapter 4, I talked about Jesus' power and authority as a gift that he desires to give to all believers. This happens through the baptism or infilling of the Holy Spirit.

Praying with Jesus' power and authority is the key to healing diseases and setting the captive free from the darkness of evil. I was never taught this basic truth growing up in church or studies at seminary. I knew that Jesus gives us his power and authority, but I really didn't understand how to apply those gifts to physical healing. During our years of exciting inner healing ministry, we would have individuals come to our healing prayer center in need of physical healing. Most individuals attending our weekly healing service would ask prayers for physical ailments such as cancer, arthritis, hearing loss, heart ailments, severe headaches and pain relief. Those prayers were always heartfelt. God's peace would surround and fill us. Many experienced healing deep hurts in their past, yet something was still missing in our prayers, in my prayers, for those seeking physical healing.

I believe that something always happens when we pray. Having someone willing to listen to our story with love and acceptance is healing. Yet it seemed only about 15 percent to 20 percent of those coming for physical healing prayer would actually experience a noticeable difference. I remember how disappointed I felt when it seemed so few were healed of their diseases through my prayers. Jesus sent out the first twelve disciples to heal the sick and cast out demons, and they did so in Jesus' name. I kept asking, "What am I missing?" I would soon find out.

Rev. Josh Acton, a friend and colleague, was the guest speaker for our 2012 annual Healing Winds Conference in western North Carolina. He taught on praying for physical healing using the power and authority that Jesus gives us. He said it was the same power and authority that raised Lazarus from the dead, that healed the lame and the blind. Simply stated, Jesus gives us his power and authority. He did this for the twelve disciples, then the seventy disciples and the disciples throughout the centuries, including Christians today. I began to realize this was my missing piece. I was not praying with Jesus' power and authority!

Heartfelt prayers are wonderful prayers, filled with love and desire for what is best for the prayer recipient. I believe we want to continue such prayers and to do so fervently. But Jesus added more to those prayers. He taught his disciples to pray "in my (Jesus') name" and to use his power and authority to bring healing wherever they encountered the sick and ailing. He never told the disciples to go out and bring the ill back to him. No! He would say, "I've given you my power and authority to heal the sick. Go and do it!"

Josh concluded his teaching of praying with power and authority, the Prayer of Command he called it, by asking if anyone in attendance was suffering from physical pain. Several individuals raised their hand. Carol was the first person Josh invited to come up to demonstrate praying for physical healing in this way. He asked her to describe her ailment. She shared that she could not lift her arm above her shoulder without experiencing intense pain. Josh asked her, "From a level of one to ten, with ten being unbearable pain, what was her present pain level? She said it was a seven.

Josh began to pray, using the prayer of command (praying with Jesus' power and authority). He prayed, "In Jesus' name, and with his power and authority, I speak to the pain in Carol's right arm and I command you pain, in Jesus' name, to release yourself from her body. Get out. Go, right at this moment." He paused and turned to Carol asking, "Do you notice any change in the level of pain. Alice, somewhat stunned, said it had gone from a level seven to about a two." Josh said a prayer of thanks and prayed the same prayer of command for the remaining pain to depart. Carol said the pain was completely gone. Josh asked her to see how high she could raise her arm. Carol raised her arm straight out above her head, completely pain free, and with joy on her face.

Josh prayed for several others who were having neck, shoulder, back or foot pain. All but one experienced pain relief. For a few there was complete pain relief while the others partial relief. We gave thanks and praise to God for the healing we witnessed. For those with partial pain relief, we prayed for the Holy Spirit to continue the healing that had begun throughout the coming night. My prayers of thanksgiving for what I had just witnessed was tempered with, "this is not how I was taught to pray. Who am I to pray so boldly, to pray with Jesus' power and authority?"

Josh and I had been like brothers for many years. I trusted him completely. I allowed my discomfort with this style of prayer, praying with Jesus' power and authority, to say: "No. This is not for me." My "no" to Jesus lasted several years, but the Lord was not going to accept this as a final answer. In the fall of 2014, I helped lead a healing ministry team to the Diocese of Durgapur located in the northeast area of India. After several days of our team teaching and equipping their clergy and lay leaders in Jesus' healing ministry, we travelled to the city of Purulia, where thousands had attended healing services in recent years. Two huge outdoor tents had been rented along with two thousand chairs. When our team arrived for the evening service, every chair was filled and people were standing two and three deep around each tent. A Spirit-filled anointing fell as we worshipped in beautiful song and dance and powerful preaching.

At 7:30 it was time to start praying. Over the last four years we had helped teach and equip over two hundred and fifty OSL India prayer ministers. What a blessing that had been for us.

When I asked the leader of their healing ministry to invite their prayer ministers to join us so that we could begin to form prayer teams, he looked at me with a surprised expression. There had been a breakdown in communication. Their prayer ministers had not been invited to attend. That left just the six of us—the visiting healing ministry team. What could we do? There were over two thousand people present and we knew that most of them had come for prayer.

I was stunned and had no idea how we would be able to pray for so many people with just six prayer ministers. If I hadn't been so overwhelmed by the situation, I might have thought about how Jesus used what was available, a couple of loaves of bread and a few fish, to feed over five thousand. I wish I had thought of that story at that moment, but I didn't. There we were, six of us, available and willing, but how, Lord? I prayed a prayer of desperation, "Help!" We formed six prayer teams each including one of our team members, an interpreter . . . and Jesus!

As I looked out over the scene, well over two hundred people were lined up at each prayer team. I began to pray for the first person, a lady suffering from back pain. I said a prayer out loud, in Jesus' name. I prayed something similar for the next couple of individuals and then paused. I whispered to Jesus, "I don't know what to do. I don't know how to pray for so many people. What do I do?" I heard Jesus say, "Pray the prayer of command. Pray using my power and authority." Desperation can be quite an incentive to help us push through our discomfort. My "no" to God quickly turned into a "yes" to Jesus.

The most prevalent prayer request was for pain relief in back, shoulder and neck from almost every woman. I asked my interpreter if this was harvest time where the women would be carrying large amounts of produce on their heads to their local markets, thinking this might be the cause of the pain. She said no, then shared that it was harvest and planting season for the rice paddies. Nearly all the planting in that area of India was done manually by women. They would be bending over five to seven hours every day planting rice seedlings. No wonder they were experiencing so much pain.

I began to pray the prayer of command for every woman experiencing back, neck or shoulder pain. *"Jesus, in your name and with your power and authority, I speak to the pain [being specific with its location] and command you to release yourself from this beloved daughter of God. Pain get out. Go. And now, I bless you in Jesus' name, with a fresh infilling of God's Holy Spirit, healing the very source of what has been causing the pain. Amen."* I then asked the interpreter to ask the prayer recipient if she noticed any change in the pain. She said, "the pain is completely gone!" The second and tenth and fiftieth woman said the same thing. I kept praying, "Thank you, Jesus. Thank you, Jesus. Thank you, Jesus."

Around 10:00, I took a quick peek to see if my prayer line was getting any shorter. After almost three hours of praying the line was just as long. It was hard to believe. I wondered if people were going from prayer team to prayer team. Bishop Dutta told me later that he observed many people leave after they received healing prayer and returned with their entire household to receive prayer! The service ended around 11:00pm. We sat down to supper tired, yet exhilarated and humbled by so many signs and wonders we had witnessed.

Because of its importance to physical healing, I have been more focused on praying with power and authority in this part of *Called to Bless*. But each prayer of command is also followed by a blessing prayer. Those blessing prayers were specific for a fresh infilling of the Holy Spirit for a particular purpose . . . healing the cause of the pain at its source. Healing prayers seek to get at the root or cause of the presenting symptoms for every individual in need of physical healing. As I look back on this experience, I became convinced God was preparing me for the ministry of blessing. And he was.

I now want to share how the Spirit has been teaching me over the last few years in blending blessing prayers with Jesus' power and authority in praying with cancer patients.

According to a recent CDC study, the rate of cancer decreased by 27 percent from 2001 to 2020. This is a very significant sign of how medical research is leading to more and more effective cancer treatments. Yet, cancer still remained the second leading cause of death, after heart disease, in the United States in 2020. There were 602,350 cancer deaths that year. These are our family members, our co-workers, our brothers and sisters in Christ. Few of us remain untouched by the tragic loss of family and friends due to cancer.

When the speaker at an OSL Healing Conference in 2015, invited anyone interested in receiving Jesus' authority over cancer to come forward, I literally leapt out of my chair. I joined the surprisingly small group gathered around the speaker. I still remember the words he prayed over us, "In Jesus' name, I bless you with an anointing of the Holy Spirit that gives each of you Jesus' power and authority over the disease of cancer."

These simple yet powerful words resonated deeply within me. I sensed the Lord's presence and said yes to receiving all the anointing he wanted to give us, to give me. By this time, I had been using a blending of the prayer of command with blessing prayers for physical healing, mostly for pain relief and for healing the cause of the pain. I also had many opportunities to teach and equip other prayer ministers in how to blend blessing prayers with Jesus' power and authority. They too were seeing miraculous signs and wonders when praying in this way. But I was seeing very little healing with cancer patients. This was about to change. The following stories reveal what can happen when blessing prayers, prayers of command, and medical treatment are combined through the leading of the Holy Spirit.

Mark's Story (cancer healed)

John, at the healing retreat at St. Johns' Church you and others prayed with me, and I would like to share some good news.

I was diagnosed with Mantle Cell Lymphoma in 2020 and had treatment in 2021. At the time of diagnosis 72% of the B cells tested were mutated in the blood they tested. I was reassessed in April 2023 with both blood and bone marrow tests this time. They could not find any of the same mutation cells in either. There was only a single mutation found which was different and not a known cancer, just a rogue cell. The doctors expected to find the cancer in the bone marrow.

I still struggle with headaches, and they are watching unrelated tumors on my thyroid grow but they are not concerned because they can remove the thyroid if the function is affected. Knowing that the 'bad' cancer is in remission is a big relief. Thank you for spreading the good news that God still heals.

Mark (Wisconsin)

Mark sent his story to me the week I began writing this section of *Called to Bless*. It felt as if God arranged the timing and wanted his story to be included to help bring encouragement to both cancer patients and prayer ministers. One of the purposes of this book is to equip others in additional ways to pray blessing prayers. With that in mind, I want to share how the Holy Spirit led us to pray for Mark.

Mark was one of the musicians helping to lead worship at the OSL Retreat. One of the retreat leaders had told me that his cancer treatments were not going well and asked if we could pray for him. I privately asked Mark if he would be open to receiving prayer from the whole group. He said yes. Following a teaching on blending prayers of power and authority with blessing prayers, I invited Mark to come up front. I then invited any of the retreat participants to come up and join us. About fifteen of us gathered around Mark. We sensed the strong presence of the Holy Spirit as we began to pray. There were many heartfelt prayers and blessing prayers spoken over Mark.

As I listened for the leading of the Holy Spirit, I began to pray, "Mark, beloved son of God, in Jesus' name I bless you with the Light of Christ surrounding and filling you. I bless you with a picture of his light moving up and down and back and forth throughout your body, acting like a divine CT scan, seeking out and absorbing tumors and all cancer and pre-cancerous cells. In Jesus' name and with his power and authority, I speak to the cancer that his invaded your body and command you cancer, in Jesus' name, to get out. Release yourself from Mark's body and go immediately into the Light that surrounds you. Mark, I now bless you with a fresh in-filling of the Holy Spirit that heals and restores you to God's good health, beginning this day and continuing for weeks and months to come. In Jesus' name I pray. Amen"

I believe there is more than one way to pray effectively for individuals, and their families, who are suffering from cancer. Where the Holy Spirit calls us to intercede, the Holy Spirit will give us words to pray, words of blessing prayers specific for the person and the disease that has invaded their body. For cancer patients, the blessing prayers and prayer of command that I was led to use began to emerge in a very simple yet powerful sequence:

1. *Prayer of Thanksgiving* for the healing God intends for the prayer recipient.

2. *Prayer of Listening* to the person's story and for the Holy Spirit's direction in how to pray. (Sometimes the cause of cancer is rooted in an unresolved deep hurt of the past where prayers of inner healing are needed first.)

3. *Blessing Prayer:* "In Jesus' name, I bless you [name] with the light of Christ surrounding and filling you with the specific purpose of searching for and destroying all cancer and pre-cancerous cells present in your body." I often add a blessing prayer for the Holy Spirit to give the person an image of Jesus' light moving throughout their body. Many individuals have said this was very helpful at the time and during subsequent prayer times.

4. *Prayer of Command:* "In Jesus' name and with his power and authority, I speak directly to the cancer and command you to get out, release yourself from [name] body and go immediately into the light of Christ that surrounds you."

5. *Blessing Prayer:* "In Jesus' name, I bless you [name] with a fresh infilling of the Holy Spirit that heals and restores all your physiological systems and function, especially cellular production. I bless you with the Holy Spirit to supernaturally strengthen and empower your immune system to fight off all disease."

(If the individual is receiving or about to start medical treatment, the following blessing prayers are important to pray.)

6. *Blessing Prayer:* "In Jesus' name, I bless your medical team with supernatural wisdom, skill and compassion for [name] and his family."

7. *Blessing Prayer:* "In Jesus' name, I bless all medications, all chemo, all radiation with the presence of the Holy Spirit enhancing the healing process with great precision and without debilitating side effects such as nausea and chemo brain."

8. *Blessing Prayer:* "In Jesus' name, I bless you [name] and every member of your family with the love and peace of Jesus flowing directly from his heart into your hearts, bringing comfort and assuredness that all will be well."

There is no magic formula, no one sequence of steps in praying for healing from cancer. Each person is uniquely created. Each person has their own specific needs for healing prayer and medical diagnosis and treatment. So, our prayers of blessing combined with prayers of power and authority must be unique for each person. How do we do this? By always beginning our prayers with a time of asking the Holy Spirit to lead us and by quietly listening for the words that the Spirit gives us to pray. Remember, Jesus said that the Holy Spirit would do this, would direct us and teach us in all things. When you and I do this, we will see Jesus' words fulfilled, *"I am telling you the truth: those who believe in me will do what I do—yes, they will do even greater things . . . "* (John 14:12).

The following story was sent by a friend gifted in blending blessing prayers with Jesus' power and authority for healing.

Blessing Mac and His Chemo Medication

Mac is the maintenance manager in our apartment complex. He's a delightful, upbeat person and beloved by all in the building.

Back in the winter he was diagnosed with rectal cancer. When he began chemo, it was administered through a port from a bag he carried around with him for several weeks. When I met him in the hallway one day, just after he was given the first bag, I prayed blessing prayers over the medication as well as for Mac's well-being. As soon as he got the second bag, he asked me to pray over that one, as well. He is now off the chemo.

After a period of losing weight and feeling (understandably) tired, he began to put weight back on and to gain strength. The reports from the doctors have been good news. A PET scan is coming up soon, and if it also is good news, he'll be able to have the port removed. During all of this, Mac has missed very few days of work.

Today, when I asked if I could send you his story, he eagerly agreed. He said he was never sick from the meds, and he said he believes the prayers made a difference.

I know I'm not the only one who has prayed for Mac's healing, but it blessed me that he asked me to pray over the second chemo bag.

Joan (TN)

Two weeks later, Joan texted me with wonderful news. Mac's PET scan showed no presence of cancer. His doctor pronounced him cancer free!

Dorene's Story (Healing from Cancer)

My journey through Pancreatic Cancer has been somewhat of a blessing. I heard God speak through scripture just when I needed it most, calming me, reassuring me that He will never leave me. He could see what was inside me and that's all I needed to know.

During the Blessing Prayer it was as though His healing light was going through my body with no stops, no blockage, or no restraints, surrounding whatever was there that should not be. God was in control and He would make the decisions freeing my body and for the chemo to go right where it was needed most. I believe in the healing power of God. I believe He uses His children to bring His word and His power to light—just as John did when he asked to pray for me—for that healing light to circulate and heal my body. God loves us and it is not his will for us to be sick.

I thank God and John for being part of my story.

Dorene (NC)

Dorene's story happened mid-morning in the church office where she worked as church secretary. As no one else was present, I asked her if this would be a good time to pray. She said yes. Dorene and I simply waited quietly upon the Lord for how to pray. I began by praying a blessing of Jesus' healing light to surround and fill her, moving up and down, back and forth like a "divine CT scan" seeking out and absorbing all cancer and pre-cancerous cells while filtering out all toxins that had been released in her body. I prayed that Jesus would bless Dorene with a visual image of his light doing this so that she could pray for his light to continue the healing process during her own times of prayer.

I then prayed with Jesus' power and authority, speaking directly to the cancer in Jesus' name: "Cancer, get out! Release yourself from Dorene's body and go into the light that surrounds you." This was followed by a blessing for "a fresh infilling of the Holy Spirit to renew and restore her back to health, to supernaturally strengthen and empower her immune system and to bring all cellular production back into its God created order, all in Jesus' name. Thank you, Lord, for your healing presence in Dorene's life!"

Impacting Dorene's healing were dozens if not hundreds of friends and family praying for her during this time while she was also undergoing modern medical treatment. Within just a few weeks of our office prayer session, her oncologist shared the joy-filled news that there was no sign of cancer! To God be the glory!

A Mother and Daughter's Healing Journey

August 26, 2022 my Mom got the phone call. "Please come to the hospital and plan to stay for 12 days. Your bone marrow test has revealed that you have acute leukemia." Her frequent response during those first few weeks of treatment, "I don't feel sick!" Over those first couple of weeks, we began to learn what fighting this disease would include: weekly blood work, transfusions, platelet infusions and chemo every four weeks.

I texted my flower farmer friend, John Rice, to share the news. Knowing he had a lot of experience in healing prayer from our "God Talk" moments at the local Farmer's Market I asked, "How do we pray?" Here is the prayer he gave me the first week of her diagnosis.

"Praying a fresh infusion of the Holy Spirit being poured into your Mom, supernaturally strengthening her immune system and releasing God's healing presence throughout her body. In Jesus' name. Amen."

A few weeks later, John called to check in with me, "How is your Mom doing? Any specific prayer requests? I replied, "Mom is home. She does not feel sick! But I think all the medications, transfusions, and appointments are getting to her emotionally. She has prayed your prayer every day! She is a very positive person. But I can tell the process is getting to her. She has to keep believing she can get well and be healthy and healed. That is my prayer today."

Mom kept praying. We had an 80th birthday celebration for her and my dad in November. The following weeks were tough. Due to the strength of all the chemo medications, she became so weak she could hardly get up out of her chair by herself. She lost weight, only 114 pounds now. She could not drive nor be left alone. By Thanksgiving we had to host our family gathering in our downstairs space because she could no longer manage the three steps into our house. I was not sure she would make it until Christmas.

John reached out to me and invited me to an Advent Retreat in Burnsville led by The Blessing Place. There were many opportunities for soaking prayer where the prayer ministers offered silent blessing prayers. Each time I requested prayers for my Mom. Within a week of this retreat, I walked into Mom's house where she was doing a weekly Bible Study with her best friend. Her face was radiant. "I feel good today!" She was so joyful and her energy had returned. It was like a heavy blanket had been removed. We were able to celebrate Christmas together.

In January, Mom's bone marrow test showed 70% less cancer. By late April, the cancer was in complete remission. She was driving again. She felt like herself. From December to August, Mom had freedom to enjoy her life. She went back to church. She enjoyed her oil painting group again. And she began to host her weekly dinners for family and friends.

August 14th she went to the Asheville Cancer Center for a checkup. Her numbers were not good. The leukemia was back. She had me sit in her chair with her when she got home. She held my hand and told me she had weeks to live. This was a hard day. She asked me to help her host two important parties for a great nephew and two special high school girls while she was still feeling well. So that is what we did.

On August 26th, I texted John, "An update on Mom. Leukemia is back. They are giving her weeks to live. She is in palliative care. I believe the prayers prayed for her at the Advent Retreat gave her an extra 9 months and counting. So grateful! It has been a bitter but sweet time of healing for our family. We are still believing in miracles!"

John felt the Holy Spirit leading him to offer to come and pray in person with Mom. She agreed and John came and prayed with me and Mom in her home. It was August 31, the day after she had gone into Hospice Care. When he asked her what she would like prayer for, she said her family. She was so worried about leaving us. John asked if she would like prayers for healing of the cancer? Mom said, "I think Jesus is calling me home, but I would stay longer if He wants me to!" John prayed a prayer of blessing of the Light of Christ to surround and fill her. Then with Jesus' authority he commanded the cancer to leave her body. I watched Mom's face tear up during this prayer and sensed the Holy Spirit doing something. John concluded the prayer and asked Mom how she was feeling, if she sensed anything happening in her body. She said that she could see light and felt the power of the Holy Spirit.

In the days that followed Mom felt like herself. We expected a dramatic decline since she was no longer receiving any labs, platelets, or transfusions. But she was still strong! The hospice nurse came to the house 5 days later to find her in the kitchen making stew and baking pecan pies for a family dinner. The hospice nurse looked at her notes and said, "You may have another one or two months at this rate. I do not see a decline."

Mom felt good. We went out that week and got a pedicure together. She walked up and down every aisle of her favorite little store. We celebrated with more family coming into town. We watched movies together, laughed, the grandkids came to visit, it was wonderful. Mom was fully alive and enjoying all of the gatherings.

On September 10, she felt a shift. We needed to get a hospital bed. Walking was suddenly harder, and her lack of platelets were causing some bruising around her eye. We gathered in closer as a family, prayed, and played music with her. We stayed with her around the clock, taking turns with her at night.

The last night I was with her, I sensed that the room was filled with light. It was much more radiant than the light bulbs in the room could provide. I did not want to leave her side. It was a beautiful time, my dad and my brother were there. At 2:45 pm September 24 my Mom was completely healed. She stopped breathing as my brother was talking to her and gave her a hug. Later, as they took her body away, I felt her speak to my spirit. "I am SO done with that body!" I felt relief, along with peace, and sadness. She was not in her little worn out body anymore. I felt like she was celebrating.

It has been two weeks since that day. It is hard to believe Mom is not here. I miss her. The past year was the hardest and the best year of my life. Mom and I became closer than ever before! We had complete relational healing. There was nothing left unsaid between us. She was more and more radiant with the love of Christ. She never complained. Even her nurses commented that she was always thinking of others and concerned with how they were doing.

During this time Mom had written in her journal many of her favorite verses and thoughts for each day. Scripture was such a lifeline for us in those past several weeks, and a treasure now as we look back on those favorite verses and small reminders of a really big God! Healing has happened in many of the lives touched by my Mom's this year. I pray that her story will continue to speak life to all of those who hear.

Thank you, John, for your faithful prayers. We truly believe Mom was given a gift of healing throughout this year and able to live fully alive all of her days!

Diane (North Carolina)

Diane's story of her mother's healing journey is such a powerful story filled with the reality of life and how God's love is always with us no matter where we are, no matter what we are facing. Her story reveals a God who heals through medical treatment, prayer and loving relationships. Healing did happen. In Diane's words, "We had complete relational healing. There was nothing left unsaid between us." What a beautiful gift for a mother and daughter!

Diane wrote, "I believe the prayers prayed for her at the Advent Retreat gave her an extra nine months and counting." What a wonderful gift of additional time to be with family and friends.

I still remember praying with Diane's mother in person that day she was placed on hospice care. She was so very weak and frail, yet her faith remained strong. Jesus was with us, filling her with more of his love and healing light, reviving her yet again. So much so that she went from hospice care to shopping and having a pedicure!

Her story also reveals the truth of these Words, *"For everything there is a season, and a time for every matter under heaven: a time to be born, and a time to die . . . "* (Eccl 3:1-2b). For Diane's mom, that time came on a Sunday afternoon in September. Diane described that moment when, "my mom was completely healed."

"Jesus, thank you for watching over mom, Diane and family during this healing journey. Thank you for welcoming your beloved daughter back home where there is no sickness, no pain, no suffering. Thank you for your continued loving and healing presence with Diane and every member of her family. Amen."

Questions for Reflection and Study

1. Many Christians are not comfortable with the prayer of command, praying with Jesus' power and authority. What do you think Jesus might say to you about any discomfort you might have?

2. Is there anything holding you back from praying with Jesus' power and authority for someone else?

3. What do you see as the significance of blending blessing prayers with prayers of power and authority?

12

Blessing Prayers to Help Get You Started

Making the Transition to Prayers of Blessing

SEVERAL YEARS AGO I began to realize that making the transition to praying blessing prayers was not an easy transition. Why? Each of us have been brought up in certain religious practices and traditions. That is true for how we are taught to pray. Many of us were taught to pray the simple yet powerful words, "God's will be done." Others, perhaps the majority of God's people, follow Pauls' instructions, *"in everything by prayer and supplication with thanksgiving let your requests be made known to God"* (Phil 4:6). It is a challenge to begin praying blessing prayers, as I have been describing, after years of praying another way.

Recently, our Blessing Place Ministry Team and I were invited to present the workshop, *"Rediscovering God's Ministry of Blessing"* at Trinity UMC in Southport, North Carolina. I had asked two members of their church to identify some of the community needs in the Southport area. We would use these for an important prayer exercise that I hoped would help individuals see the difference between blessing prayers and the ways they had been praying.

Each workshop participant was instructed to select one of the community needs—family, church mission, domestic violence, addictions, etc. I then asked them to write a prayer as they normally would in response to the need they had chosen. When they had written their prayer, I then asked them to take their prayer and turn it into a blessing prayer. Here are a few of their prayers. Note that the second prayer for each need is the blessing prayer.

> *Dear Lord, my heart is so broken by the hatred and division we now see in our country and our world. How do we change this, Lord? What do I do to make a difference? Oh God—HELP!*

> *In Jesus' name, I bless our nation and our world with Your Light, Your Grace, Your Peace and Your Love. I pray in Your Name that all will see Your Truth, feel Your Love, and turn from Self to Selflessness, to know that we ALL are children of God, made in His image. Let there be peace on earth—and let it begin with me.*
>
> Marlou

> *Dear Lord, give Diana and Loretta strength and comfort as they fight the cancer that is in their body. Be with the health care team using their knowledge and gifts to provide support and comfort. In Jesus' name. Amen.*

> *In Jesus' name I bless Diana and Loretta with strength and comfort from the Holy Spirit as they fight the cancer in their body. In Jesus' name I bless the health care teams with knowledge, empathy, wisdom, and courage.*
>
> Debbie

> *Dear Lord, you know how I'm feeling, at 83. I feel old and weak, don't know what my purpose in life is anymore. Please give me a reason for living! In Jesus' Name, Amen.*

Dear Lord, thank you for leading us here today. In Jesus' Name, I bless myself. Thank You for loving me and having a plan for my life. Thank You that You're not done with me yet! In Jesus' Name, Amen.

Betsy

Father, please protect the children and teachers in our schools. Protect them as they ride the bus, as they play and as they learn. Please protect them from all evil. In Jesus' name, Amen.

In Jesus' name, I bless the children, teachers, bus drivers and all staff of our schools with Your protection from all evil. I bless them with Your Holy Spirit guiding them. I bless the adults to see every child through Your eyes and to love them with Your love. Thank You, Lord, Amen.

Kim

Abba, my family is lost. My sister and brother are sad, angry, unforgiving and I want them to know you! I want them to know your great love and grace, Your deep mercy. Flood them with each, Lord. In your Holy name, Jesus, Amen.

In Jesus' name I bless my brother and sister with joy, peace and forgiveness. I bless them in Jesus' name with a deep desire to know you! I bless them in Jesus' name with Your great love and grace and Your deep mercy. I bless them with a flood of Your Holy Spirit power, in Jesus' name. Amen.

Debbie

As I read these prayers for the first time, I was struck by how each was so heartfelt. All the prayers are quite good, reminding me that we are given multiple ways to intercede for one another. Notice what makes blessing prayers different from the prayers of request that can be found in the examples above. Each blessing prayer begins with, "In Jesus' name, I bless." Each one places a greater focus on specific outcomes (or God's intentions for each need). Each blessing prayer carries a greater sense of praying with Jesus' authority.

How do you know when to use blessing prayers? Listen for the leading of the Holy Spirit. And get ready to be led more and more to pray blessing prayers.

God's ministry of blessing is growing exponentially. The Holy Spirit is leading the way and equipping God's people throughout the land. The blessing prayers in this chapter are meant to be a jumping off place to help you in your journey of being *Called to Bless*. It is an invitation to wade into the waters of blessing ministry. Jump on in. The water is life-giving.

A Call to Blessing Ministry

When I first heard about blessing prayers from John, I was entranced by the beautiful simplicity of them and I decided to give them a try. I started out by writing a simple blessing, *In Jesus' Name, I bless you with the love of God, the joy and peace of Jesus, and the powerful Presence of the Holy Spirit*, which I spoke to people whenever I felt God was nudging me. I blessed my doctor, the air conditioner repair man, the garbage collector, the clerks in stores and my friends and family. No one ever turned me down when I asked if it was ok if I blessed them—in fact, they seemed delighted to be blessed. They always left with a smile and thanks. The more I blessed people, the richer, deeper and more personal the blessings became, and I discovered that I was blessed in return whenever I spoke a blessing. Speaking blessings has become a way of life for me now, and I'm so thankful for John's teaching!

Occasionally I have felt God leading me to write out a blessing prayer for someone special or for a special occasion, and to speak it over the person and then give them the written copy. I wrote one for my nephew's ordination, one for my granddaughter when she graduated from college, for the closing of healing conferences, and other times as God has led me. Each time, I felt a specific nudge to sit with God and allow Him to guide me in writing a prayer to bless the recipient. After a time of waiting in silence for His leading, the words flowed into my heart and onto the paper—words of encouragement and affirmation, words of love and hope, and words that spoke of God's wonderful plans for their lives. The look of joy on their faces as they received the blessings was so rewarding. I was hesitant when I wrote the first one, but the positive response I got gave me confidence to try again, and again, and again. I discovered once again how faithful the Holy Spirit is to help us when God calls us to serve Him, and what a blessing it is to be able to share God's heart with His children.

Ditsie (Merritt Island, FL)

Blessing Prayers written and used by Ditsie

"In Jesus' name, I bless you to be filled with the love of God to fill any dry places you have had in your life, and to overflow to those around you. I bless you with the joy of Jesus to bubble up within you to vanquish the darkness around you, and the peace of Jesus to be with you no matter what circumstances you find yourself in. And in Jesus' name, I bless you to be full of the powerful presence of the Holy Spirit to teach you and guide you into all He has for you. Amen.

In the name of Jesus, I bless the people of [church name] with a powerful infilling of the Holy Spirit, and a new openness to his working among us. Amen."

Blessing for a Ministry

"In Jesus' name, I bless you with a richer prayer life and greater intimacy with God, with peace that passes all understanding, with faith to move mountains, with extravagant praise, and the ability to stand firm in the face of trials. I bless you to be filled with the enveloping, saturating love of God, with the bubbling joy of Jesus, and with the sweet, presence of the Holy Spirit.

In Jesus' name, I bless you with empowerment and cour-
age as you serve the one who loves us all, with opportunities to
minister to the broken and the lost, and with an abounding hope
that fills your heart, your mind, and your soul. I bless you with
grater anointing in the healing ministry—with hands that heal
and a heart that loves, with eyes that see into the spiritual realm
and ears to hear the quiet voice of God.

In Jesus' name, I bless you to flourish in the fullness of all that
God has planned for you. I bless you with boldness to go where
he sends you and a willingness to be used by him. I bless you with
Holy Spirit power and the wisdom of God.

In Jesus' name, I bless you with a deeper relationship with
Christ, with the love of God to bring every cell in your body alive
in him, with the joy and peace of Jesus to be with you no matter
what you're going through, with the powerful presence of the Holy
Spirit to guide you as you pray with others, and I bless you to be
filled with living water that flows from God's heart through yours
to those he brings to you. In Jesus' name. Amen."

Blessing Prayers for an After School Children's Program

Here is how I usually start praying for kids I work with
in the After School Program at our church. Father, in
the name of Jesus, I bless [name] with his heart being
prepared by You, like good soil, so that the seeds of truth
planted there will take root and grow and bear much
fruit—fruit unto salvation. I bless [name] to know in the
deepest place of his inmost being how high and wide and
deep and long is Your love for him. And I bless [name]
with the conviction of the Holy Spirit to know how much
he needs you. Open his spiritual eyes, Lord, to see you
working in his life and open his spiritual ears to hear
Your voice calling him and guiding him. Amen.

Kim (NC)

High School Graduation Blessings

"[*Niece's name*], in Jesus' name, I bless you with a summer filled with joy and laughter. I bless you with wonderful friendships, friends that you can trust and who will always be there for you. I bless your college choice to be just right for you in both educational opportunities and location (meaning a little, to a lot, of hockey!). I bless you with the wisdom and discernment of the Holy Spirit to guide you in all your decisions, both small and large. I bless you with continuing to grow into all that God has created you to be. I bless you and your family with the Lord's protection in all that you do and wherever you are. And [name], I bless you with the love of the Father, the peace and joy of Jesus, and the power and truth of the Holy Spirit this day and every day. All in Jesus' name. Amen!"

Questions for Reflection and Study

1. What do you see as the differences between how you have been praying and the blessing prayers written in this chapter?

2. What do you like most about the blessing prayers in this chapter?

3. What individuals and/or situations in your life would benefit by your speaking blessing prayers into those needs? Is there anything that would prevent you from doing so?

13

Blessing Prayers for Church and Community Needs

WHEN THINKING OF A chapter on using blessing prayers that bridge church and community needs, I thought of the experiences of The Blessing Place at the Mission Abbey, a ministry of All Saints Anglican Church in Jackson, Tennessee. The following is their story, as written by The Rev. Terry Blakely, a leader and visionary for their ministry. It is a wonderful story of how the Holy Spirit has led them in bringing God's blessing ministry into their church and local communities. I am hopeful their story will be a source of encouragement and inspire you to seek your own unique ministry of blessing in your church and local community.

"Blessing God's People in the Name of Jesus"

"If there's a God, he surely doesn't know my name."

"I'm bad to the bone, ma'am. God ain't gonna forgive the things I've done."

"I try to pray to God, but my prayers go no further than the ceiling."

"Jesus? Who's that?"

Everyday people going about their everyday lives. All of us. We need God, but for many, he seems so far away. We wonder, "Why would God want to have anything to do with the likes of me?"

We, The Blessing Place at the Mission Abbey, have found that blessing prayers can be a bridge to the loving presence of God. God's Holy Spirit will set up divine encounters for blessing prayer. He will prompt and direct the conversations and prayers and they will be life and love affirming.

As you and your prayer team move out in blessing prayer, be open to the leading of the Holy Spirit who inspires delightful and creative ways to bless others in the name of Jesus. This happened one day to our prayer crew. We had a blast, a blessing blast!

Blessing Blast

What would do you do with fifty fresh, gloriously beautiful red roses left over from a church event? Drop them off at a nursing home or at the home of an elder shut-in? Leave them in the church for next Sunday's service, hoping the roses will still be fresh? "But Jesus," we asked, "is there something else you would have us do with these roses? How could we use these roses to bless the people today in your name?" We asked. We waited. We listened. And off we went on our first blessing blast!

We loaded the roses into a car and wondered, "Where should we go?" What should we do? Our initial thought was to go to a local grocery store. We would ask the manager for permission to give each employee a rose and a quick prayer of blessing, thanking them for their service. But as we headed in that direction, we felt the Holy Spirit nudging us away from the grocery store and toward a busy breakfast café. We prayed aloud, *"Pat's Place? Is Pat's Place where you want us to go, Lord?"* We felt nudged in that direction. So we drove to Pat's Place, not sure what we were to say or do. Would we be well received, or chased away by a harried manager during this busy breakfast hour? A little nervous, a little excited, we were already on an adventure with the Lord!

Upon arrival, we grabbed half of the long-stemmed roses and walked into the café. Within the first ten seconds, a waitperson passed by, eyeing the bundles of flowers in our arms, saying, *"Ooh, I hope those roses are for me!"* *"Well, actually, they are,"* we replied with a big smile, and asked to see the manager. We told the manager that we appreciated all the good, hard-working people who worked at Pat's Place, and that we wanted to thank them by giving each a rose and a blessing. The manager seemed surprised, saying that nobody had ever done anything like this before. She went on to describe the long hours that she and her staff worked, then called serving staff members one-by-one to receive a rose and a blessing from us.

Each encounter with a staff member was a short burst of blessing! The Holy Spirit paved the way for quick, intimate communication about life's hurts, situations and needs of help from God. One said, *"We're mostly invisible here; thank you for caring about us."* Another said sadly as she took the rose, *"my grandmother just passed away; this rose is for her."*

We expressed our thanks to each one, saying that we had seen their hard work and kind service to customers. We noted their cheerfulness despite the many hours they work every day. We assured each one that the Lord God was with them in their troubles and cares. We asked permission to say a quick prayer of blessing over each person. No one refused. Some hugged us as we prayed for them, while others shared prayer needs with us in tears. Some expressed that no one had ever prayed for them before, and they were grateful.

When we were done, the manager asked if she could give a rose to each of the line-cooks working in the back kitchen (*"the young men back there have girlfriends and wives who would appreciate a rose,"* she said). We were delighted, giving her roses for every person who worked at the eatery. We said a quick prayer of blessing over the manager and the café and thanked her with a rose of her own. We left the restaurant in a cloud of glory. This blessing blast had taken about ten minutes from start to finish.

We were filled with wonder and gratitude to God for ushering us into this joyful experience.

We were energized over this first blessing blast experience, and wondered what we were to do next. We still had twenty-five roses. "*Where next, Lord? The grocery store?*" No! We felt directed to the pancake house just ten minutes away. So, off we hopped to another popular breakfast haven, a little anxious, but leaning on the Holy Spirit to lead the way. Walking in with armloads of roses, we experienced much the same response at this second establishment as the first. It was wonderful. The manager was kind and helpful, and we prayed for about as many employees there as previously. However, we had three roses left. Where was the Lord going to send us next?

As we walked out of the restaurant, a customer waiting for his takeout order, said under his breath, "*I wish I had one of those roses to give to my wife.*" We stopped in our tracks, turned to the young man and said, *"and so you shall! Here! They're yours! Take these roses for your wife!*" The man seemed a little embarrassed that we had overheard his wish and tried to pay us for the roses. We insisted that he take all three, explaining that it was our way of asking God to bless him. So, he took the roses with many expressions of thanks.

He told us that times had been hard of late, and that the roses would mean a lot to his wife. We sat down beside him to hear more of his story, all of which pointed to his deep devotion to his wife and three children. With his permission, he allowed us to pray God's blessings over him and his family. He bowed his head as we prayed blessings of provision, health, harmony, and godly wisdom over him and his family. The joy of that holy moment is hard to describe, but we felt Heaven come down all around us on that humble bench where people come to wait for food. We were out of roses, but we were filled with joy!

Since that time, we've done a number of blessing blasts. Where have we conducted other blessing blasts? A steak house at the dinner hour, a mental health clinic for adolescents, an office supply store, a walk-in medical clinic, a nursing home for veterans, a walking park, a city dump depot where we prayed blessings over the attendant there, a retirement village, and a mental health professional group at a local university. We have yet to go to a grocery store, but we suspect the Lord to direct us there eventually. His timing. His plan.

God wants to bless and wants us to bless. When we step out in faith on a blessing blast, we are doubly blessed. We get to be on mission with Jesus to demonstrate his love for people through our hands, feet, eyes, ears, and voice! Intimacy with Christ increases as we experience these divine encounters. Our capacity to tap into the leading of the Holy Spirit is enhanced, and we are energized and encouraged to tell others about God and his desire to bless and save.

Notes on Blessing Blast Ministry:

The rules of the road for carrying out a blessing blast include keeping things simple, short, safe, and respectable. We operate in pairs, praying as we go, asking the Holy Spirit to lead us to the people and places he has prepared, and to inspire what we say and do during the encounter, taking care to:

1. *Ask* permission from the manager of the establishment to proceed in the actions of thanking, giving, and blessing.

2. *Thank* the manager for their time, leaving gracefully if the manager refuses our request.

3. *Respect* individuals as we approach them, thanking them for their specific service to others and the community; we then ask permission to pray a blessing over them after giving what tangible gifts we have for them; if our offer to pray for the person is denied, we kindly say "no problem" and move on.

4. *Appreciate* the establishment as a place of business and service, understanding we are guests requesting a favor; we take great care not to interfere with the peace and operation of the establishment.

5. *Keep* the blessing blast encounter short, ten minutes or less!

Themed Blessing Services

While our prayer team loves to do blessing blasts, we realize there are people who are experiencing challenging seasons of life, who may feel alone and unsupported in hard circumstances, or who simply want a blessing encounter with God. Once a quarter, the prayer crew hosts a blessing service at our church to uplift, honor, and pray specifically for people who identify with the theme of the service. The wider community is invited so all can experience God's grace and mercy. The services are short, informal and provide time and space for quiet reflection, and private and corporate prayer.

We have developed four themed blessing services: *The Blessing of the Burdened, The Blessing of the Children, The Blessing of the Marriages,* and *Blessed Are Those Who Mourn.* If you would like a detailed description of these services, please contact the Rev. Theresa Blakely at All Saints Anglican Church in Jackson, Tennessee.

Final Thoughts

Healing prayer is blessing prayer. Blessing prayer is healing prayer. The two go hand-in-hand. At least, that is what our prayer crew has realized—that we can hardly pray healing over a person without praying God's blessing over them as well.

When someone comes to us in need of <u>healing prayer</u>, we pray God's blessing of healing, peace, wisdom, strength, life, support, provision, understanding, divine guidance, and spiritual and physical wellness over the person.

When one comes in need of <u>blessing prayer</u>, even if it is for a blessing specific to a need, we still pray God's blessing of healing, peace, wisdom, strength, life, support, provision, understanding, divine guidance, and spiritual and physical wellness over the person.

If you are reading this, I suspect you are experiencing a nudge by the Holy Spirit to God's ministry of blessing. As you lean into this holy call with your own crew of praying friends, ask Jesus to guide you in how to jump-start your own blessing prayer ministry. He will answer you in surprising and creative ways, showing you how to approach all kinds of people who are hurting and in need of God's saving embrace. Lead with the love of Christ for others in your heart, and you can't go wrong. Life is short. Get to it!

Theresa Blakley, Deacon

The Blessing Place at the Mission Abbey All Saints Anglican Church, Jackson, TN

Questions for Reflection and Study

1. What stood out to you as you read the story of The Blessing Place at the Mission Abbey?

2. Would a themed blessing service be something you would like to see offered in your church? What would the theme be? What next steps are needed for this to happen?

3. What do you think about doing blessing blasts in your community? What would such a blessing blast look like for you and your team? Where would you go?

14

Your Journey Begins

As I WRITE THIS last chapter, I'm looking out the window in my study, gazing at the beauty of God's creation. The ridges of the Southern Appalachian mountains are in the distance, backlit with the pastel pinks of a late autumn sunset. The mountain slopes are covered with a dusting of snow, the first of the season. We are in the midst of seasonal change, from fall to winter. This is when The Blessing Place of Western North Carolina was conceived, during the fall and winter months of 2017.

I believe that becoming a People of Blessing begins with a calling, a Call to Bless. The first step towards your ministry of blessing begins with gathering. It is a gathering of those in your local area whose hearts have begun to hear the Call to Bless. It is a gathering whose primary purpose is to pray and wait upon the Lord to receive His vision for your ministry of blessing.

This is what we were called to do at the Blessing Place for a period of seven months. We prayed silently for fifteen to twenty minutes and then shared what we had heard and seen with each other. Some groups will take far less time, others more. The length of time it takes to receive this vision is far less important than your willingness to wait upon the Lord, where you will receive the vision for what God's ministry of blessing is to be for you.

Know that your willingness to seek God and wait upon him in prayer aligns so well with the words of Jeremiah, an Old Testament prophet. *"Then when you call upon me and come and pray to me, I will hear you. When you search for me, you will find me; if you seek me with all your heart"* (Jer 29: 12). When you do this you will not only find God, you will also discover (discern) God's plans for your blessing ministry. *"For surely I know the plans I have for you, says the Lord, plans for your welfare and not for harm, to give you a future with hope"* (Jer 29: 11).

Wait upon the Lord. Seek God with all your heart. There is no better place to begin your blessing ministry, designed by God with Jesus as your ministry cornerstone. Your work in doing this builds the foundation for an effective, sustainable, life changing ministry of blessing as only you and your team are uniquely created to do. It is time to move forward with the ministry of blessing. I hope the following prayer will help you do just that.

In Jesus' name, I bless you (and your group) with a fresh infilling of the Holy Spirit that will lead and direct you in all areas of your blessing ministry. I bless you with a gifting of all the spiritual gifts, especially gifts of discernment, wisdom and healing, needed to birth and grow your ministry of blessing. I bless you with all the skilled and faithful co-workers you will need to come alongside you at just the right time. I bless you with the love of God flowing directly from Abba's heart into your hearts. I bless you with Jesus' overflowing peace and joy. And I bless you with the light of Christ surrounding you, your ministry team and all your families, protecting you from all harm, all sickness throughout the working hours of the day and resting hours of the night. In Jesus' name I pray. Amen!

Questions for Reflection and Study

1. Are you feeling "called to bless"? Are there others you know who feel the same?

2. Do you have friends (church, neighborhood, at work) with whom you would enjoy doing blessing ministry? How would you go about inviting them to join you?

3. What are the next steps for you (your group) in creating or expanding God's ministry of blessing in your community, your church?

APPENDIX

Ministry Resources

(All Ministry Resources found in the Appendix may be used without seeking the author's permission.)

Praying with Jesus' Power and Authority

1. Jesus used the Prayer of Command in over half of his twenty-six healing miracles

   - For physical healing (*"be clean, stretch out your hand, get up and walk"*)

   - For deliverance of evil spirits (*"be quiet, come out of him"*)

2. Rooted in God's power and authority

   - Begins with Jesus "full of the Holy Spirit" (Luke 3:22, 4:1, 4:14; 4:18-21)

3. Jesus gives his power and authority to his disciples to heal and to preach the gospel

   - to the twelve disciples (Luke 9:1)

   - to the seventy (Luke 10:1, 8-9)

– Jesus gives the same power and authority to believers today!

4. Use Prayer of Command only when you discern the Spirit's leading to pray in this way

   – Especially with physical healing and deliverance prayers

   – Seldom used for healing hurts of the past

Key Steps—Using the Prayer of Command for Physical Healing

1. *Listen to the person's request and brief history regarding the pain.*

   – Take just a few minutes for this step. Ask a few brief questions regarding the pain.

   – When did the pain begin? Was it due to an injury?

   – Ask the individual about the pain level they are experiencing right then, with ten being excruciating pain and zero being no pain. This helps give them a way of measuring the pain level as it decreases through prayer!

2. *Share with them that you will be using the Prayer of Command.*

   – Explain that it is prayer using Jesus' power and authority for healing.

3. *Pray the Prayer of Command, taking no longer than a few minutes.*

4. *Take a "time-out" or just pause from praying and ask them if they notice any difference.*

   – Ask, "Has the pain decreased any or is it still the same?" "What is pain level now?"

   – Do not be discouraged if the pain level is the same. Jesus teaches us to persist. Give thanks for the healing (by faith) and use Prayer of Command once again.

- If the pain has decreased any at all following first or second Prayer of Command, be encouraged, give thanks and pray Prayer of Command a third time.

- Conclude prayer session with blessing prayers for the Holy Spirit to continue the healing process during the coming night and day.

A Prayer Using the Prayer of Command

(for physical healing)

"Lord, I give you thanks and praise for your beloved daughter/son. I thank you for the healing that you desire to give (person's name.) Praying in Jesus' name and with his power and authority, I speak to the pain in (person's name . . . knee, hand, back, etc.) and command it to release itself; to get out right at this moment and go quickly and quietly to Jesus. (Person's name), I now bless you with a fresh infilling of the Holy Spirit to heal what has been causing the pain you have been experiencing. Thank you, Lord, for the healing that you are bringing to (person's name) at this very moment. Thank you, Jesus. It's in your name I (we) pray." AMEN.

1. Continue to pray the Prayer of Command, as the Spirit leads, checking in with the individual after each time the Prayer of Command is used for changes in pain level.

2. Conclude with prayers of thanksgiving and for the Spirit to complete the healing that has begun.

3. It is important to personalize the Prayer of Command, praying the words the Spirit gives you. Always pray in Jesus' name and with his power and authority when using the Prayer of Command!

4. Be sure to conclude with additional words of blessing as you are led.

Soaking Prayer Healing Service (Liturgy)

WELCOME

SINGING

WORDS OF GATHERING

Leader: We come in this service to God,

All: *In our need and bringing with us the needs of the world.*

Leader: We come to God, who has come to us in Jesus,

All: *And who walks with us the road of our world's suffering.*

Leader: We come to God, who has sent to us the Holy Spirit,

All: *bringing into the world God's power to heal,*
renew, and restore.

Leader: We come with our faith and with our concerns.

All: *We come with our hopes and with our fears.*

Leader: We come as we are, because it is God who invites us
to come,

All: *And God has promised never to turn us away.*

SCRIPTURE READING & REFLECTION

CONFESSION OF SIN

Leader: God forgives and heals us.

All: *We need your healing, merciful God:*

Give us true repentance.

Some sins are plain to us;

Some escape us, some we cannot face.

Forgive us; set us free to hear your word to us;

Set us free to serve you.

Leader: God forgives us.

Forgive others.

Forgive yourself. Amen.

THE LORD'S PRAYER

Our Father, who art in heaven, hallowed be thy Name,

thy kingdom come, thy will be done,

on earth as it is in heaven.

Give us this day our daily bread.

Forgive us our trespasses as we forgive those who trespass against us.

And lead us not into temptation but deliver us from evil.

For thine is the kingdom, and the power, and the glory,

for ever and ever. Amen.

PRAYER OF INVITATION

Leader: Like the first disciples whom Jesus instructed

to wait for the gift of the Holy Spirit,

we wait quietly, in faith, as we pray:

All: *Be with us, Holy Spirit;*

nothing can separate us from your love.

Be with us as of old, fill us with your healing power,

direct all our thoughts to your goodness.

Be present, Holy Spirit;

bring faith and peace, wellness and wholeness.

> *Thank you, Holy Spirit,*
>> *for your loving presence in our lives.*

ANOINTING OF PRAYER MINISTERS
(Prayer ministers come forward to have their hands anointed with oil.)

SOAKING PRAYER HEALING INSTRUCTIONS

- those attending the service are asked to remain in their pews (seats)
- prayer ministers will come and stand behind you to pray quietly
- if you are not comfortable with laying on of hands, please sit forward
- individuals are asked to have their prayer request cards filled out using the blank side of the 3 x 5 card in your bulletin
- please have the cards where the prayer ministers can read them
- the service lasts about one hour
- individuals are free to leave earlier if needed